Porcelain Garden

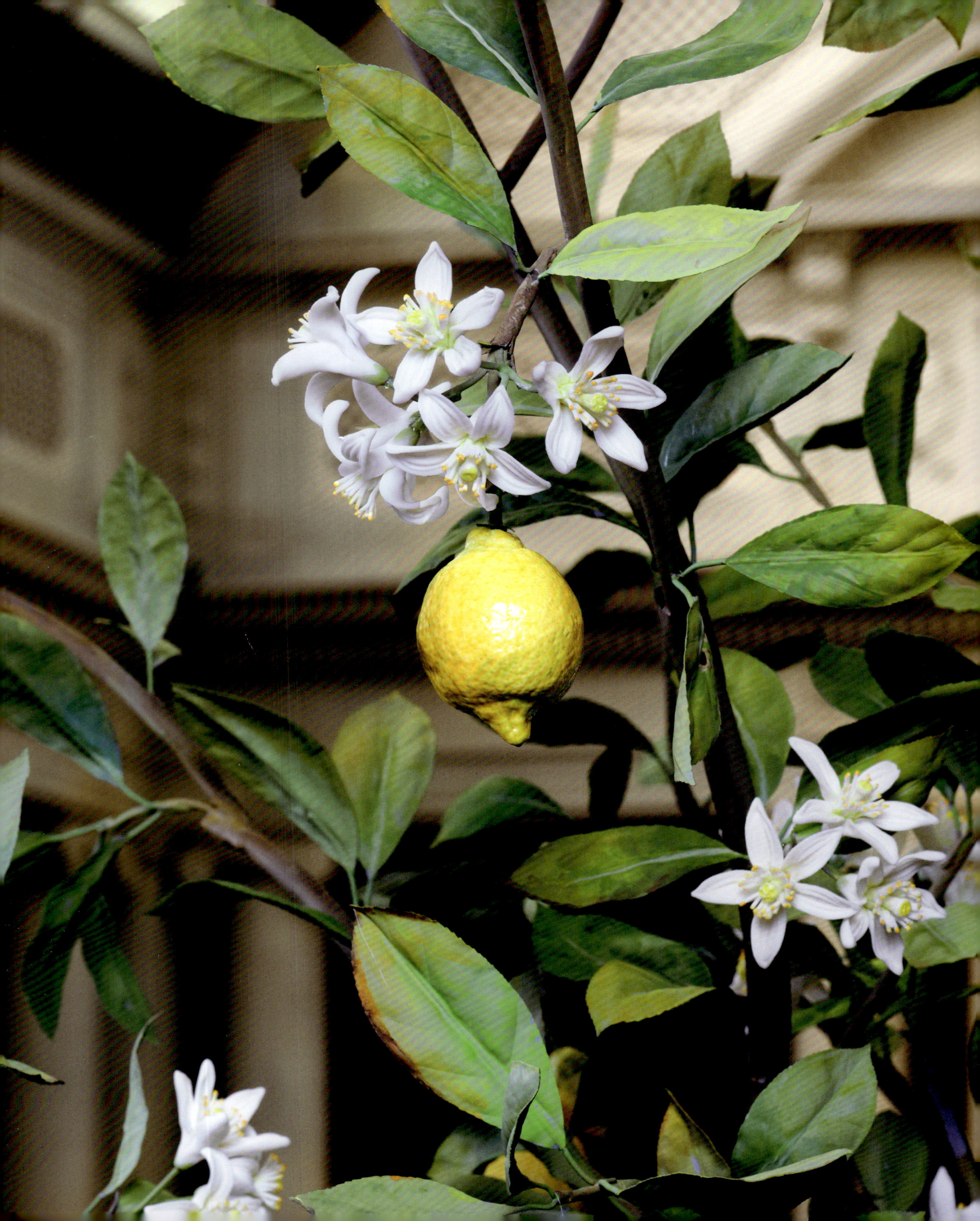

Porcelain Garden
Vladimir Kanevsky at The Frick Collection

Xavier F. Salomon

The Frick Collection, New York
In association with D Giles Limited

This catalogue is published on the occasion of *Porcelain Garden: Vladimir Kanevsky at The Frick Collection*, an installation on view at The Frick Collection from April 17, 2025, to October 6, 2025.

This installation is made possible through the generous support of Mr. and Mrs. Charles M. Royce, Ellen A. Michelson, Douglas Dockery Thomas, Winifred A. Baker, Patricia Dugan Perlmuth in memory of Bill Perlmuth, Mr. and Mrs. Lionel Goldfrank III, and Dr. Nancy Simon.

First published in 2025 by The Frick Collection

1 East 70th Street
New York, NY 10021
www.frick.org

In association with GILES
An imprint of D Giles Limited

66 High Street
Lewes, BN7 1XG
United Kingdom
gilesltd.com

Michaelyn Mitchell, Editor in Chief
Gemma McElroy, Assistant Editor

Designed by Luke Hayman and Antonio Nogueira, Pentagram New York
Printed and bound in the United States

Cover and frontispiece:
Vladimir Kanevsky, Lemon tree, 2024–25.

A CIP catalogue record for this book is available from the Library of Congress.

Image Credits:
Fig. 2. GmbH & Co. KG / Alamy Stock Photo
Fig. 3. © The National Gallery, London
Fig. 4. Photo Allen Phillips
Fig. 5. © President and Fellows of Harvard College
Fig. 6. Photo Andrey Terebenin and Svetlana Ragina

ISBN: 978-1-917273-16-9

Contents

Director's Foreword & Acknowledgments

THERE ARE NO visual records of the flower arrangements that adorned many of the Frick's key spaces when the museum opened to the public in 1935, but one can imagine the beauty of the sprays orchestrated by Henry Clay Frick's daughter, Helen Clay, as they comingled with the extraordinary art on view. With fresh flowers no longer permissible in the galleries, Xavier F. Salomon, Deputy Director and Peter Jay Sharp Chief Curator, conceived of the idea of recreating the feel of those flower arrangements with porcelain flowers by the gifted sculptor Vladimir Kanevsky.

Vladimir began his career working as an architect in St. Petersburg, making a turn to porcelain after he immigrated to New York in 1989. He was drawn specifically to flowers not only because he had always enjoyed studying botany in school, but because he liked their structure, comparing it to that of a good building. We are profoundly grateful to Vladimir for his extraordinary generosity in making some thirty exquisite arrangements for the Frick and to Xavier for his ingenuity in initiating the commission.

Others at the Frick whom we wish to acknowledge are curators Aimee Ng, Giulio Dalvit, and Marie-Laure Buku Pongo, who worked closely with both Xavier and Vladimir on the installation. Jenna Nugent, Head of Curatorial and Exhibitions Projects, oversaw every stage of the process and aided in its success in innumerable ways. Editor in Chief Michaelyn Mitchell managed the production of this catalogue and, with Assistant Editor Gemma McElroy, expertly edited the text. Joseph Coscia Jr., the Frick's photographer, is responsible for the terrific photography. Others to whom we extend our thanks include Tyler Beard, Tia Chapman, Allison Galea, Lisa Goble, Joseph Godla, Caitlin Henningsen, Patrick King, George Koelle, Alexis Light, Sara Muskulus, Christopher Roberson, Heidi Rosenau, Justin Samson, April Kim Tonin, and Sean Troxell. The entire staff had a hand in making this remarkable installation a reality, and our gratitude goes to them all. We are also indebted to lighting designer Anita Jorgensen and her team and Luke Hayman and Antonio Nogueira of Pentagram for their beautiful design of this book.

Finally, we wish to extend our gratitude to those whose generous support has made this installation possible: Mr. and Mrs. Charles M. Royce, Ellen A. Michelson, Douglas Dockery Thomas, Winifred A. Baker, Patricia Dugan Perlmuth in memory of Bill Perlmuth, Mr. and Mrs. Lionel Goldfrank III, and Dr. Nancy Simon.

Axel Rüger
Anna-Maria & Stephen Kellen Director
The Frick Collection

Porcelain Garden
Vladimir Kanevsky at The Frick Collection

ON DECEMBER 16, 1935, when The Frick Collection opened officially to the public, the key spaces on the ground floor were adorned with fresh flowers. These were meticulously chosen by the founder's daughter, Helen Clay Frick. Ten days earlier, Helen Clay had relayed the specifics of her selections to the museum's first director, Frederick Mortimer Clapp. The West Gallery was to be decorated with a vase holding thirty-six large American Beauty roses. The Library was to have a bowl of a dozen red camellias and Talisman roses. Two small vases with lilies of the valley were to be in the Fragonard Room. The Boucher Room—which had been moved from the second floor to the first to make it available to the public, when the second floor was turned into offices—was to be adorned with two small vases of lilies of the valley and forget-me-nots. For the Living Hall, yellow roses were selected, as well as a vase of mimosas for the room's center table. In some cases, Helen Clay chose flowers in relation to specific works of art. Placed under Titian's *Portrait of a Man in a Red Hat*, a bowl with a dozen anthuriums linked the color and shape of the flowers to that of the subject's hat. Some of the flowers she wanted were not available. For instance, the quince blossoms and forsythia she requested for either the Living Hall or the West Gallery were both out of season. The florist (Consolidated Florists Co. at 792 Madison Avenue) noted, "Miss Frick is more anxious to have Quince Blossom in either the living hall or large gallery, but I am not sure as to whether or not this will be ready in time for the opening." Unfortunately, no photographs survive of the opening of the museum, and there are no records of the flower arrangements. In the following years, fresh flowers were on display in the galleries on a regular basis (*fig. 1*).

The idea of incorporating flowers into the Frick's momentous 2025 reopening, following its expansion and renovation, arose early on. This was inspired largely by the desire to have flowers in the galleries, as was done in 1935. However, today's conservation practices for works of art in the collection preclude having fresh flowers in the galleries, so an appropriate replacement had to be found. The plan to fashion a series of porcelain flowers for most of the key spaces developed in the last three years, through conversations between Vladimir

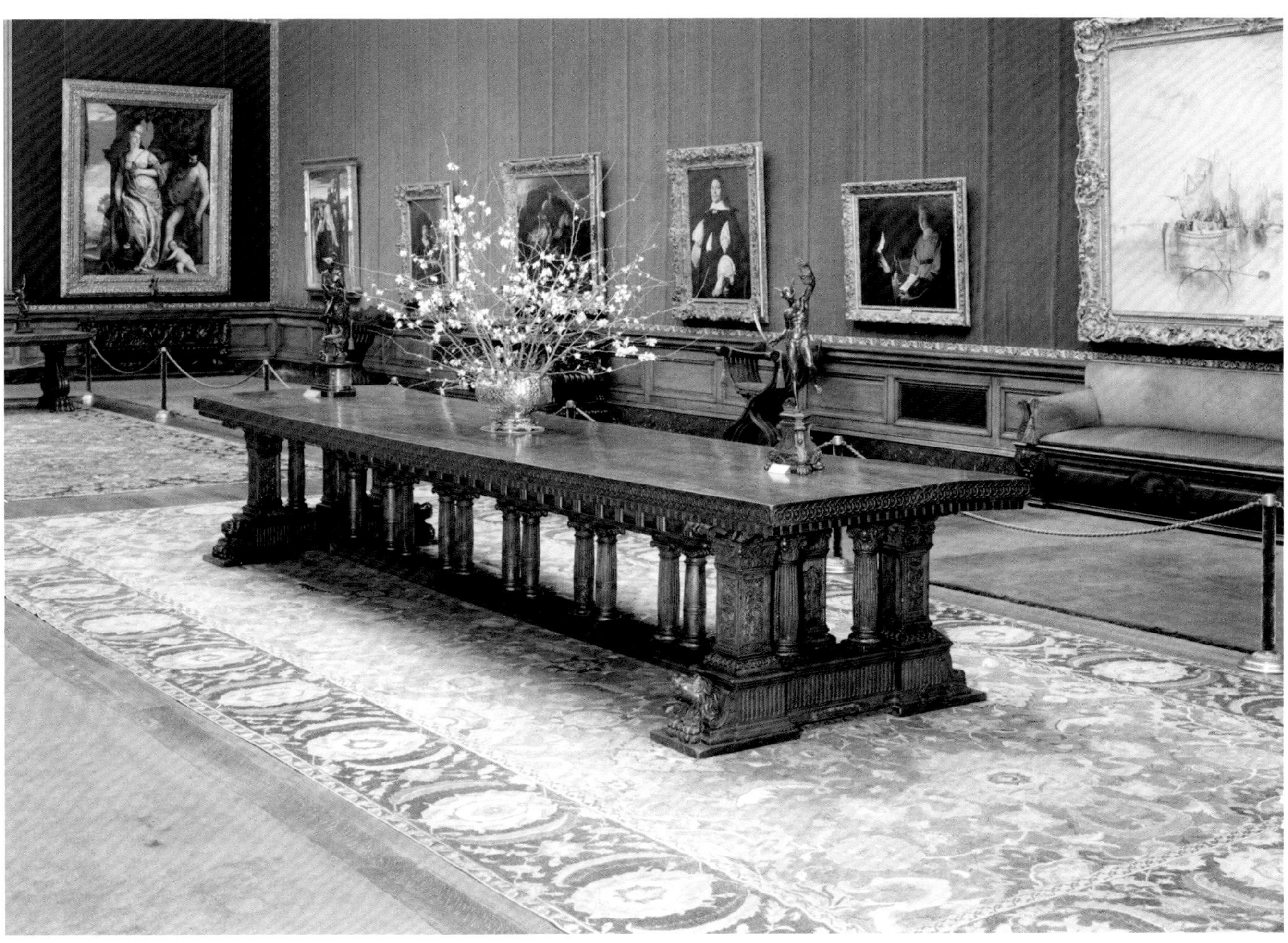

Kanevsky and the Frick's curatorial team. Some flowers are arranged in vases and pots as cut flowers would be. Others are placed on floors and surfaces in a more natural way. The locations are central to this project. Kanevsky's flowers inhabit the Frick mansion as its owners and staff did between 1914 and 1931 and as visitors do today, each creation eliciting surprise and enjoyment.

In most cultures, milestone moments—from birth to marriage and through to death—very often include flowers in one way or another. The language of flowers has developed across centuries and geographical boundaries in endless ways, with specific flowers holding varying meanings. In Japan, for example, chrysanthemums signify nobility, longevity, and rejuvenation. They are the emblem of the imperial family and, as such, almost a symbol of the country itself. In Europe—especially France, Spain, Italy, and Poland—chrysanthemums are associated with death and are therefore seen at funerals and in cemeteries. In Europe, marigolds are linked to the Virgin Mary and are used as offerings to her (hence their name), whereas in Mexico, they are linked to the Day of the Dead. In Europe, white lilies are connected to the Christian scene of the Annunciation and are therefore seen at weddings. They are also used in wedding ceremonies in Asia, where they are symbols of fertility.

Flowers have been depicted in art since antiquity. Among the oldest depictions of flowers in bloom are those from ancient Egypt. On a number of stones in what is called the "Botanical Room" or "Garden Room" in the Temple of Karnak at Luxor, an anonymous sculptor carved in relief representations of flowers that the Pharaoh Thutmose III brought back to Egypt from his military campaigns (*fig. 2*). In European art, especially in paintings, still lifes of flowers developed as a genre, particularly in the seventeenth and eighteenth centuries. Flowers in paintings were most popular in Italy, Spain, and the Netherlands, with artists focused on bouquets in vases, often combining flowers that in nature bloomed in different seasons (*fig. 3*).

A desire to replicate flowers three-dimensionally, both artistically and for scientific purposes, developed in the early modern period. Among the many materials used were papier mâché, metal, glass, and porcelain. In eighteenth-century France, Madame de Pompadour, longtime mistress of King Louis XV and a towering tastemaker in Europe at the time, was a devotee of flowers and gardens, and also of Asian and European porcelain. It was not until the 1710s that Europeans—in Meissen, Germany—discovered the formula for making porcelain, which until then had been imported from Asia. Madame de Pompadour was the patron of the first French porcelain manufactory, at Vincennes, in the 1740s, and of its renowned offspring at Sèvres. One of the most celebrated creations at Vincennes are bouquets of porcelain flowers, structured on metal stems and with metal leaves (*fig. 4*). In this way, the celebrated gardens of Pompadour's many houses entered her mansions through objects that defeated the biological transience of flowers.

Between the mid-1880s and 1936, Czech artist Leopold Blaschka and his son Rudolf created more than four thousand specimens of glass flowers, accurately depicting more than eight hundred species of plants. The Blaschkas were based in Hosterwitz, near Dresden, and worked on their glass flowers as a commission for the Botanical Museum of Harvard University. Here, the goal was a scientific one—to replicate as closely as possible the natural examples (*fig. 5*).

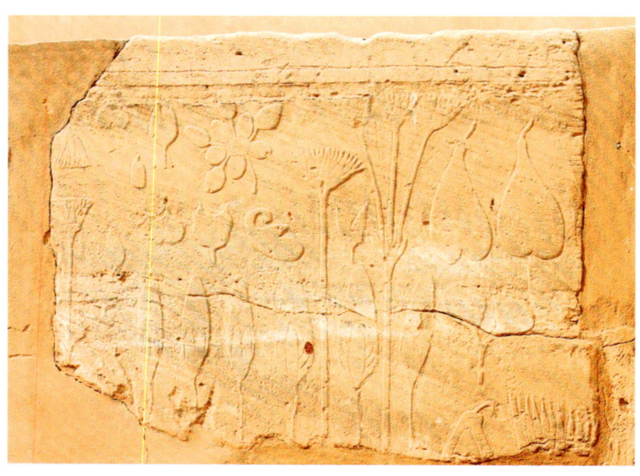

Fig. 2.
Botanical Garden of Thutmose, III, Temple of Karnak, 15th century BCE
Luxor, Egypt

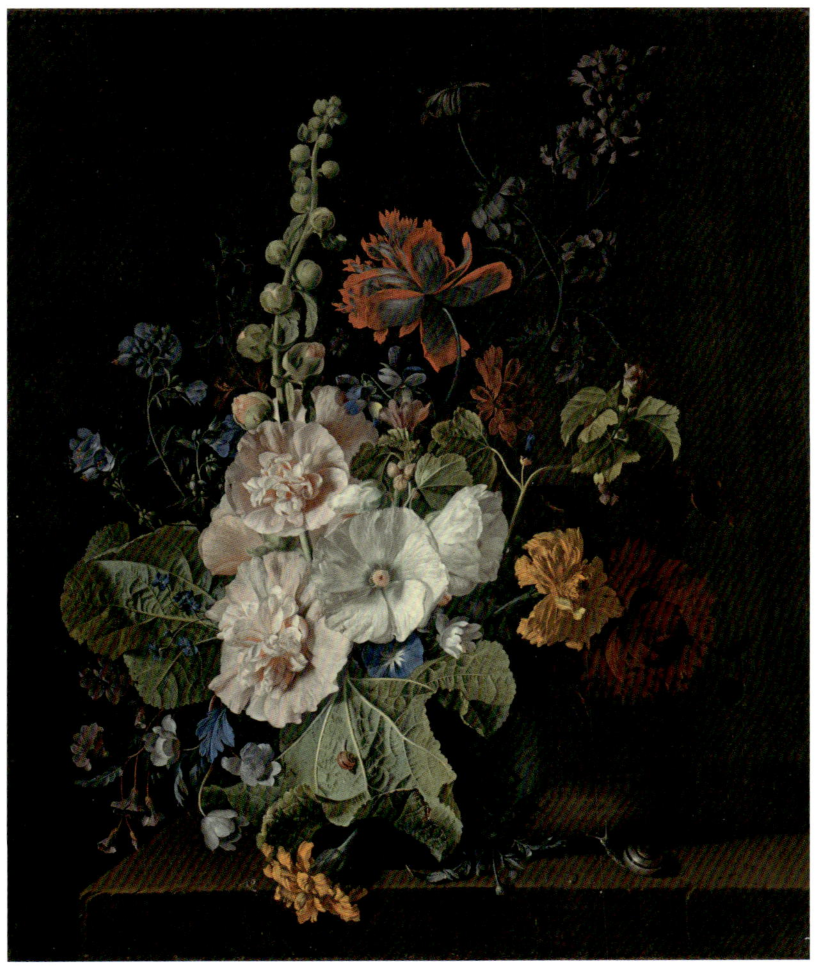

Born in Kharkiv, Ukraine (then part of the Soviet Union), Vladimir Kanevsky studied architecture in Russia and afterward became a figurative sculptor. Both architecture and sculpture are fundamental to his approach in creating his porcelain flowers. Each piece is architectural in conception, envisioned as a structure that inhabits space. The sculptural quality of each piece goes hand in hand with this underlying approach.

After immigrating to the United States, where he has been based for thirty-five years, Kanevsky began to create his flowers. These are by no means simple representations of natural flowers—though he does aim for accurate depiction—but artistic interpretations, in the same manner as a still life by Jan van Huysum or a vase of porcelain flowers made at the Vincennes manufactory. Over the years, Kanevsky has interacted with the long tradition of producing works of art in porcelain. This is best exemplified in a series of pieces created and exhibited at the Meissen manufactory in 2012.

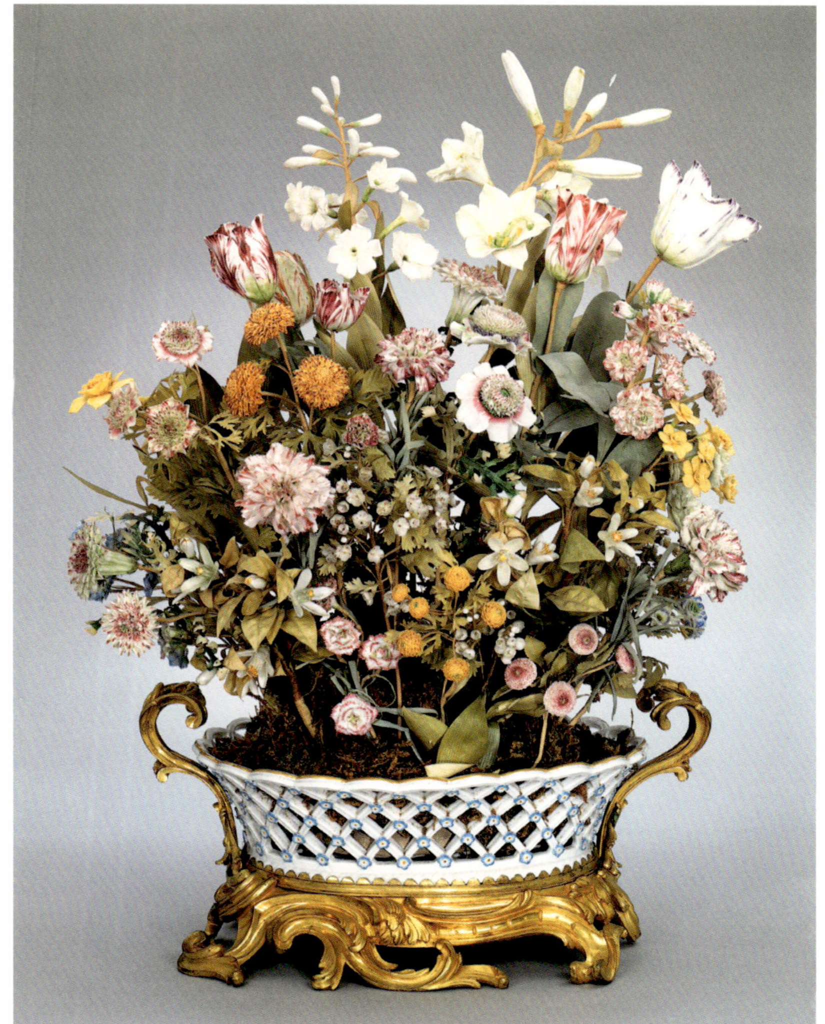

In 2017, Kanevsky also exhibited his work at St. Petersburg's Winter Palace, once the residence of the czars and now part of the State Hermitage Museum (*fig. 6*). While the flowers were in a palatial building decorated for generations of the Russian imperial family, his pieces were displayed in a museum setting, the fragile flowers encased in glass vitrines. A few years later, in 2021, Kanevsky created more of his flowers for the Hillwood Estate, Museum and Gardens, in Washington, DC.

The large bouquet of Kanevsky lilacs in the Frick's Dining Room—placed at the center of the table and surrounded by portraits by Gainsborough and Romney—is like one Helen Clay may have commissioned from the florist. In other cases, such as the white roses in the Fragonard Room, Kanevsky has responded directly to the paintings. The porcelain roses, in front of mirrors, echo the painted ones

12

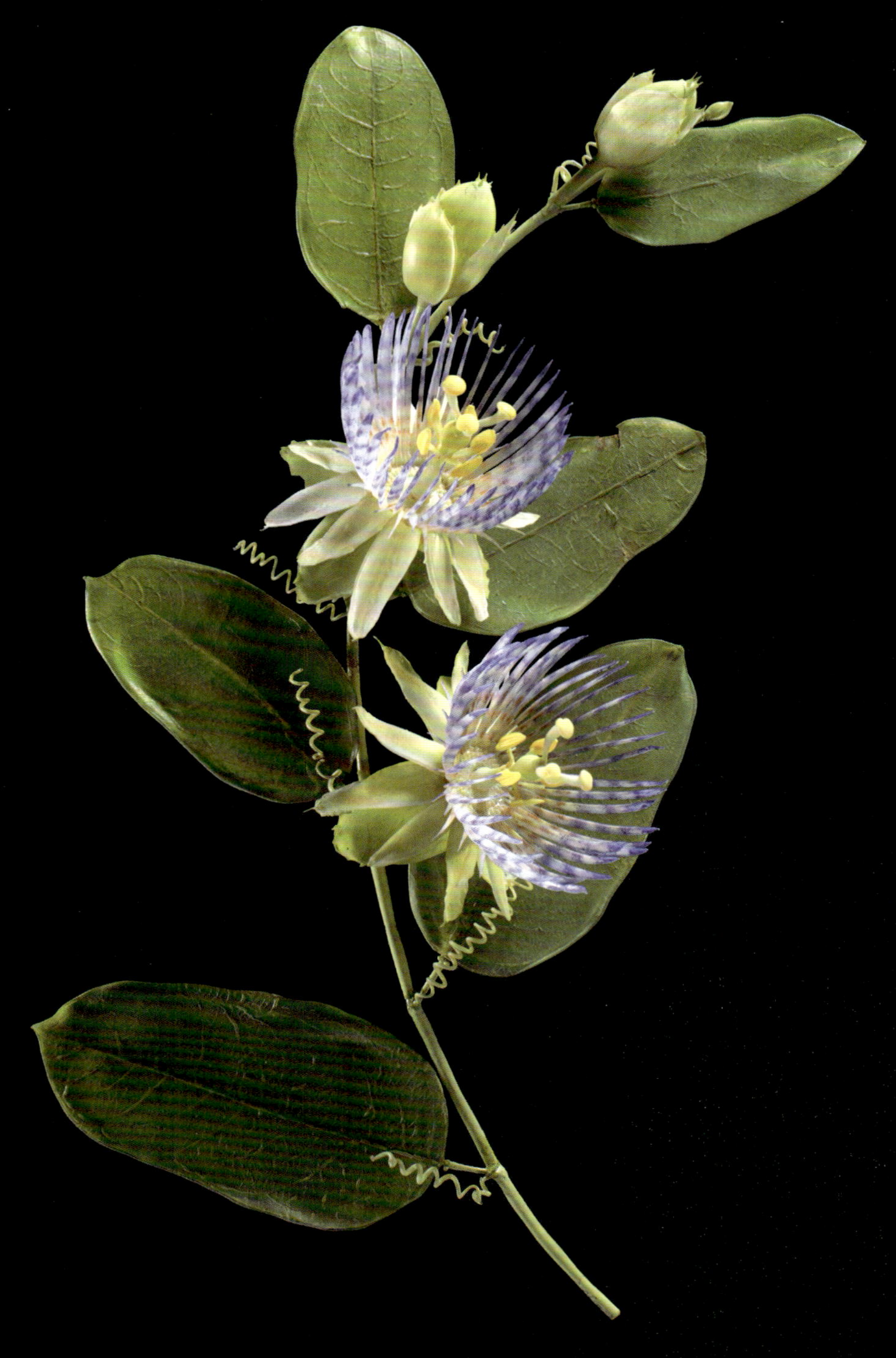

Fig. 5.
Glass model of Passiflora laurifolia by Leopold and Rudolf Blaschka, 1893. The Ware Collection of Blaschka Glass Models of Plants, Harvard University Herbaria / Harvard Museum of Natural History

cascading from Fragonard's *Progress of Love*. The flowers constitute conversations between Kanevsky's art and the Frick's collection.

Large peonies and camellias are placed on the tables in the West Gallery and Library. In only two cases—the camellias in the Library and the lilies of the valley in the Boucher Room—has Kanevsky replicated Helen Clay's choices for the 1935 opening. The plants and flowers selected often connect to specific works of art. For instance, the pomegranate tree in the Gold-Grounds Room is a tribute to a plant whose fruits are often represented in early Italian paintings. Even though no pomegranate is visible in the Frick paintings by Cimabue, Duccio, Paolo Veneziano, Piero della Francesca, Gentile da Fabriano, and Fra Filippo Lippi, this is a fruit all these painters would have known and depicted. The large, wild artichoke plant under Giovanni Bellini's *St. Francis in the Desert* is meant to conjure the wilderness of the saint's retreat at La Verna. In some cases, ceramic pieces from the Frick's collection are used to contain Kanevsky's works, as with the large faience planter from around 1680, made in Nevers, France. Designed to hold and display citrus trees, it is now in the Garden Court with a large porcelain lemon tree in it—its fruit and flowers prominently shown. Porcelain tulips are presented in the tulip vase from the Du Paquier Manufactory, made in Vienna around 1725 and displaying a charming view of the Austrian capital.

On the Frick's second floor, now for the first time opened to the public, Kanevsky's porcelain flowers inhabit some of what were the Frick family's most private rooms. Nowhere is this more poignant than in the Walnut Room, once Henry Clay Frick's bedroom. This is where Frick died on December 2, 1919, surrounded by the warmth of the walnut paneling and possibly gazing at George Romney's *Lady Hamilton* as "Nature." Overlooking Central Park, pots of black poppies celebrate Frick's gift of his collection to the public but also strike a melancholy note in the celebration of the museum's reopening.

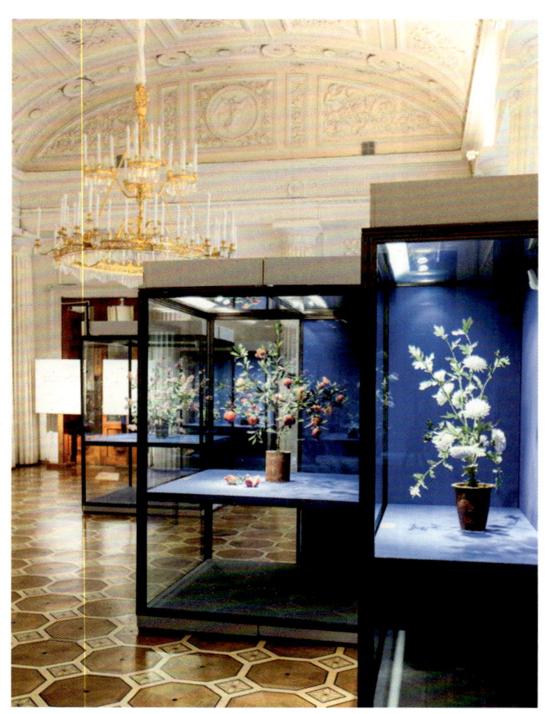

Installations

All works were made by Vladimir Kanevsky in 2024–25.
The mediums are, variously, soft-paste porcelain, bone china,
parian body, black porcelain, glazes, copper, and terracotta.
Photography is by Joseph Coscia Jr.

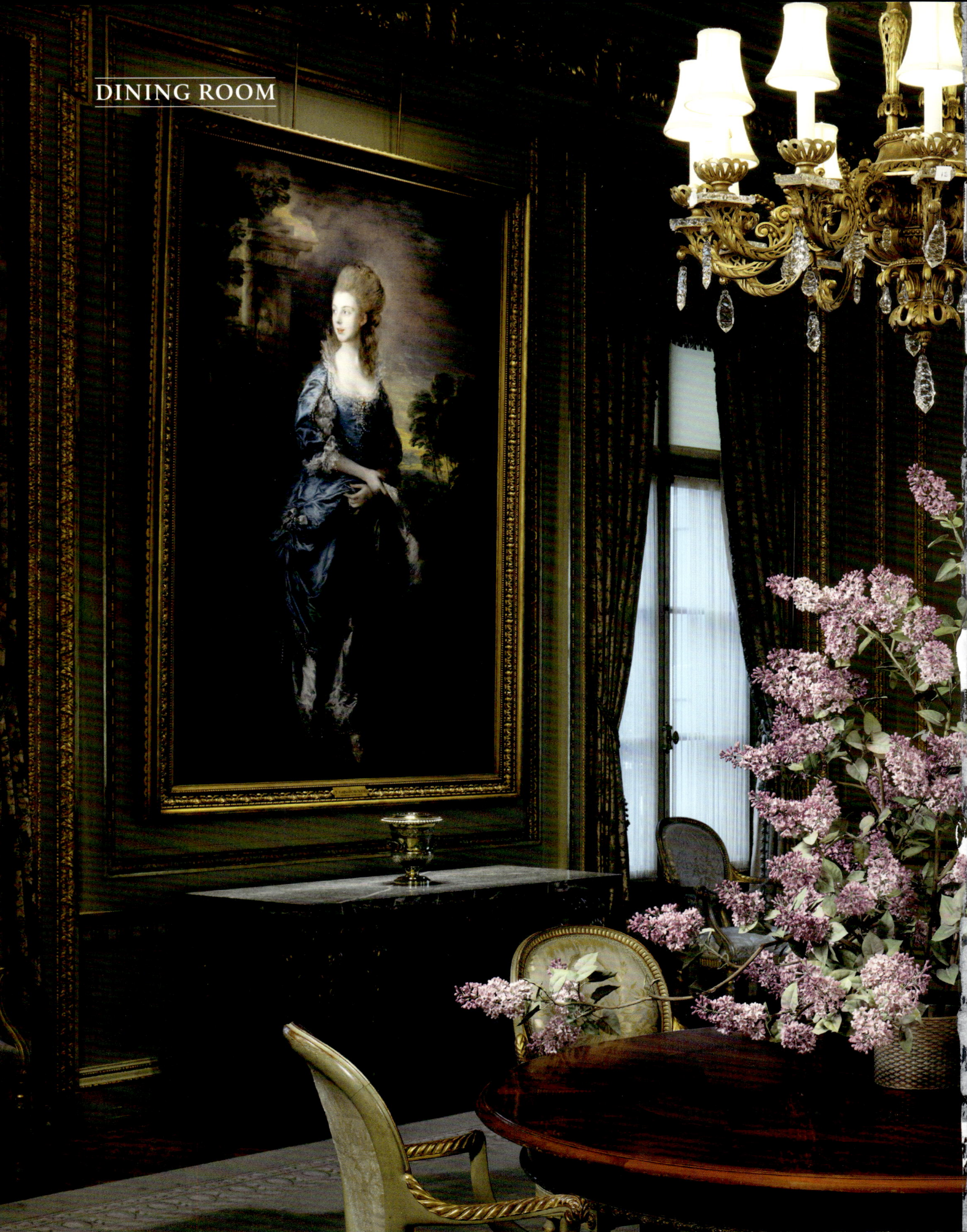
DINING ROOM

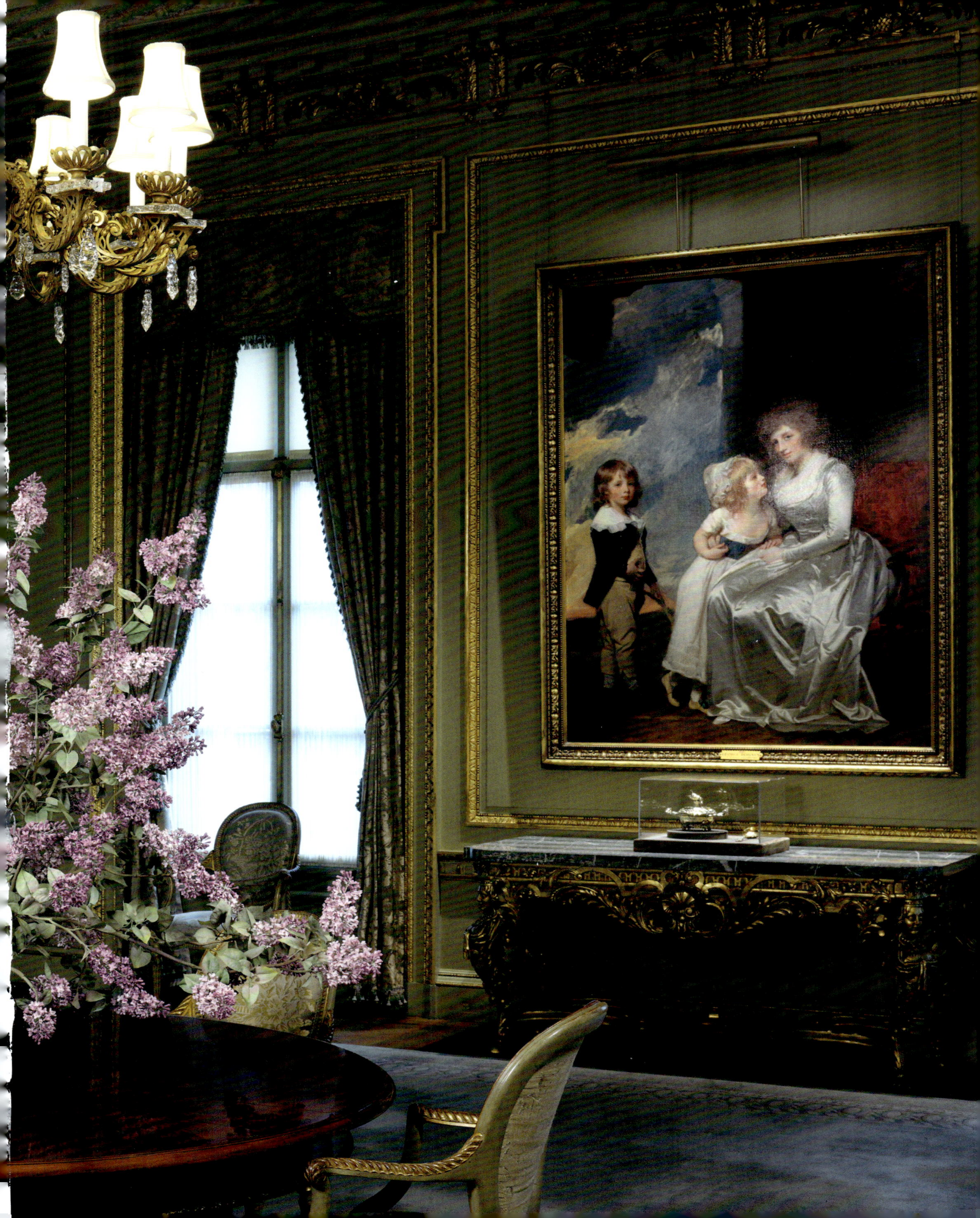

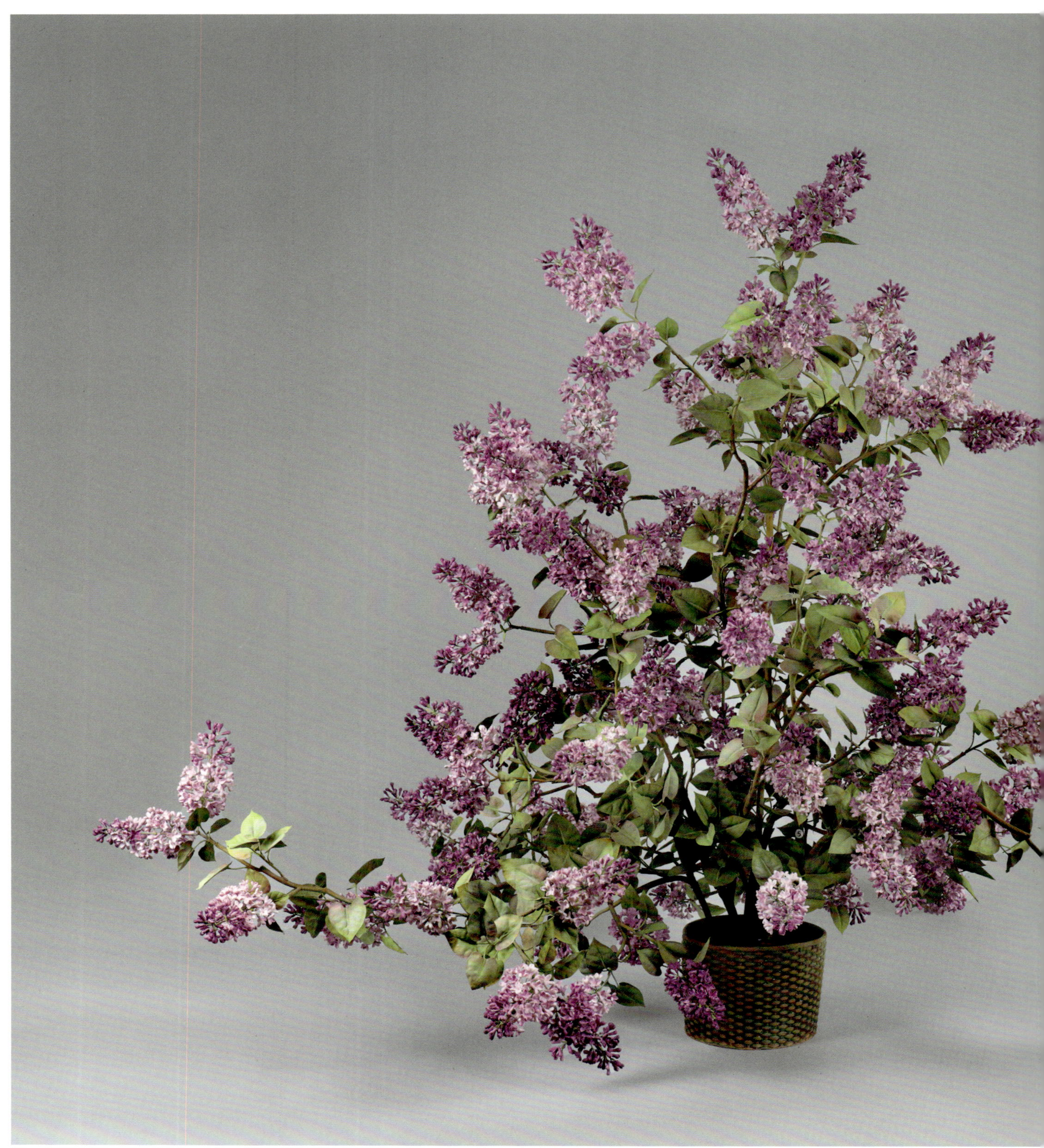

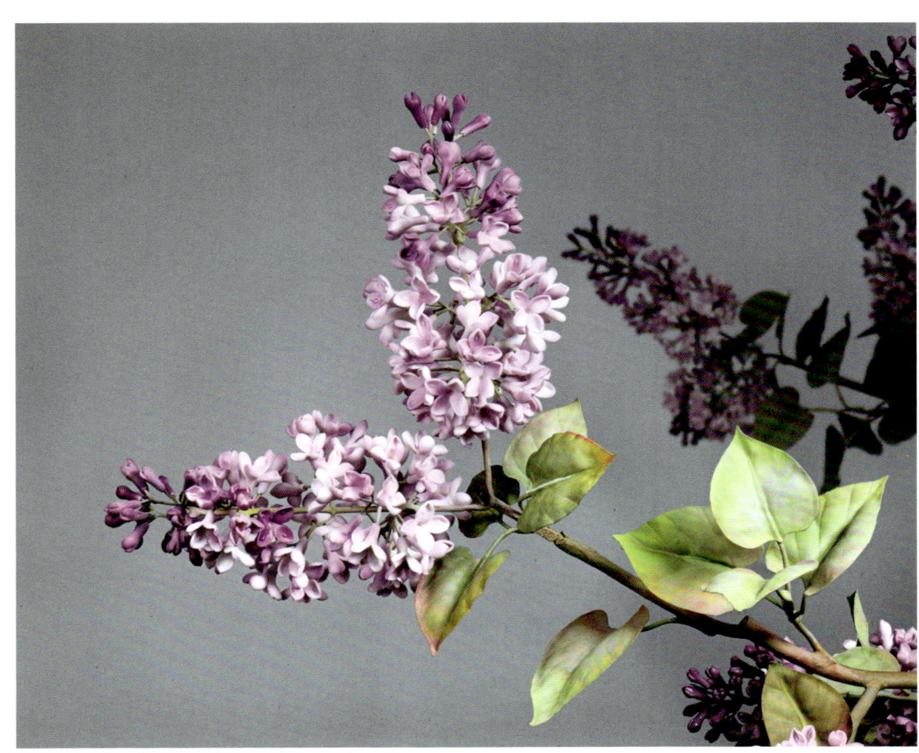

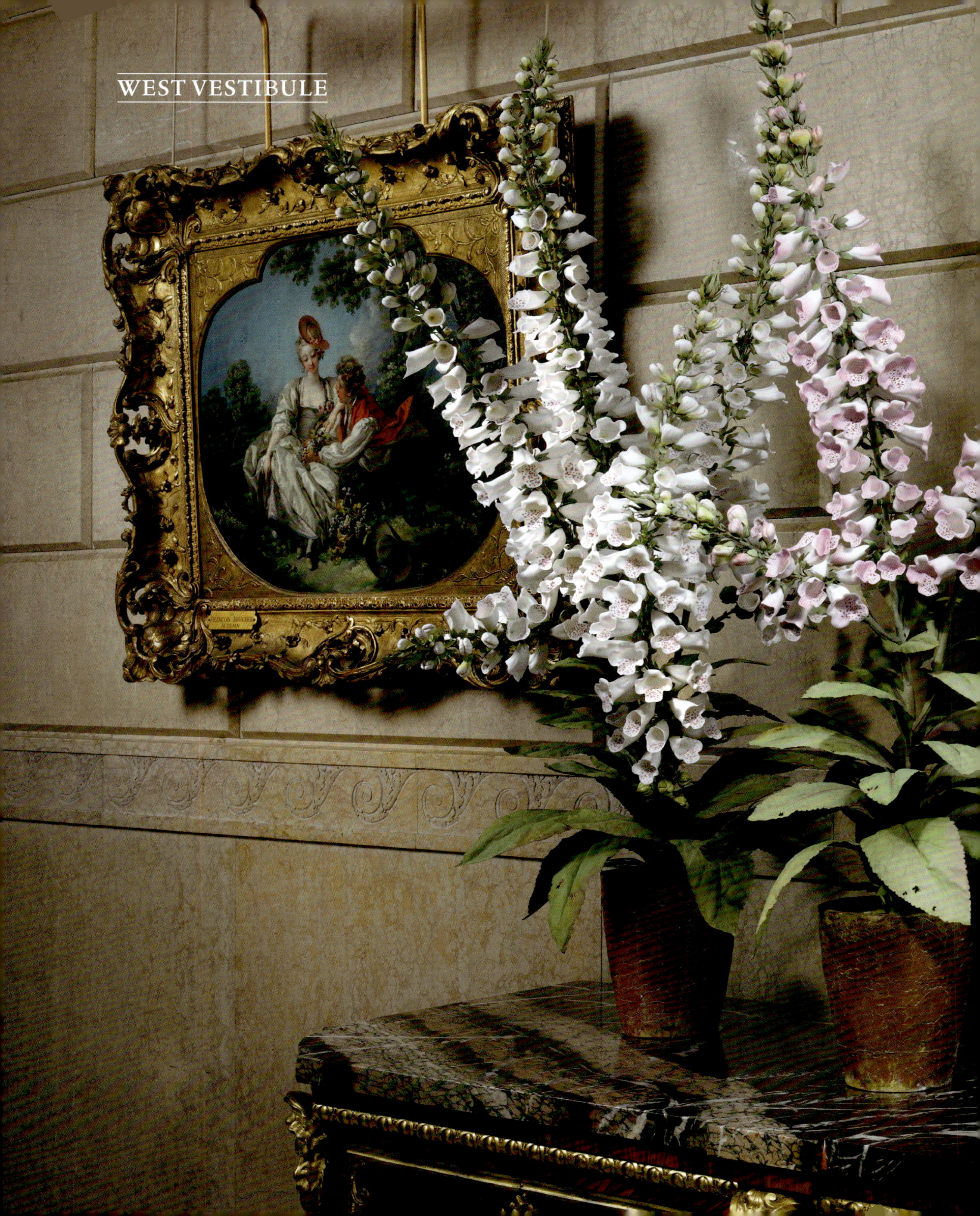
WEST VESTIBULE

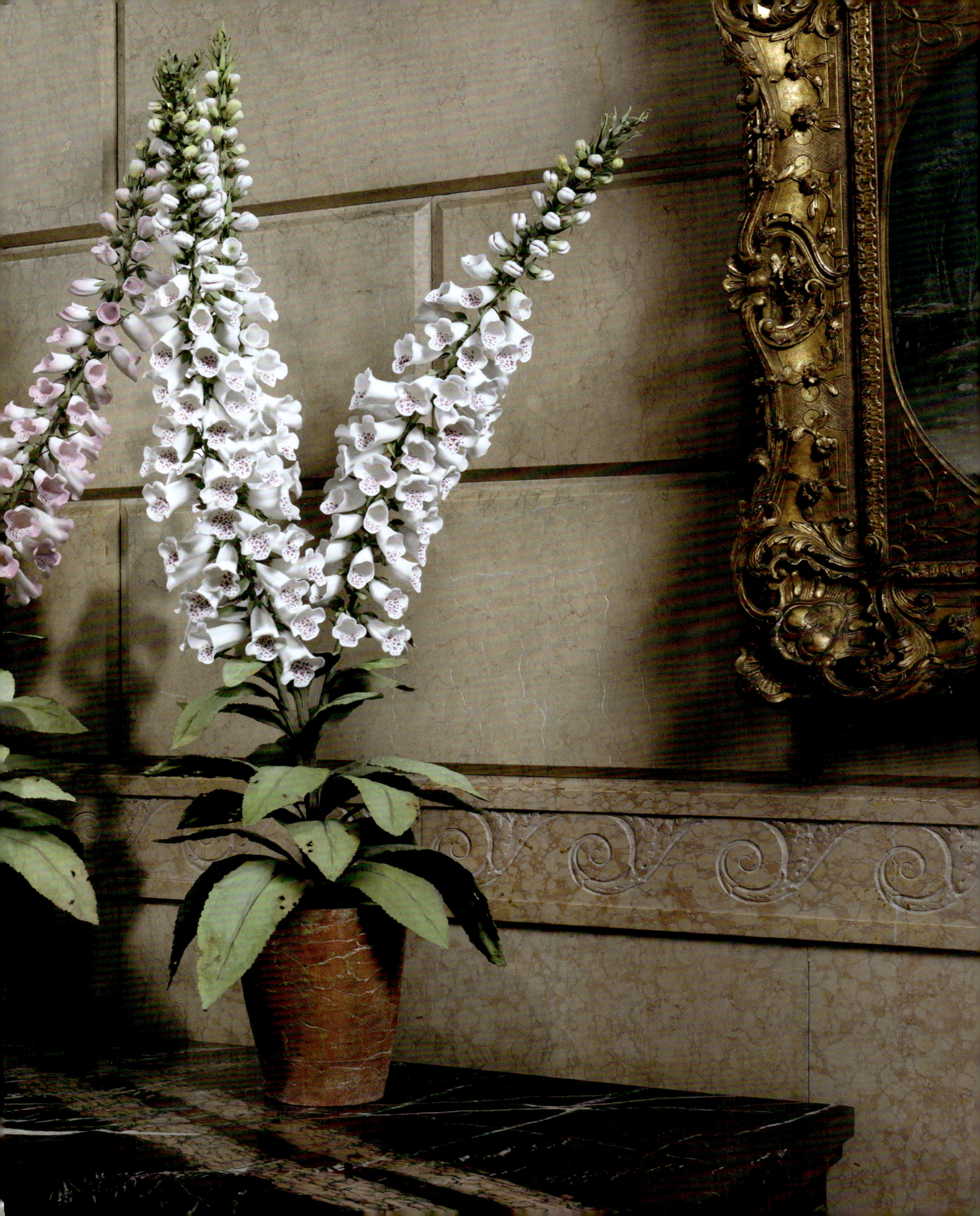

Foxgloves

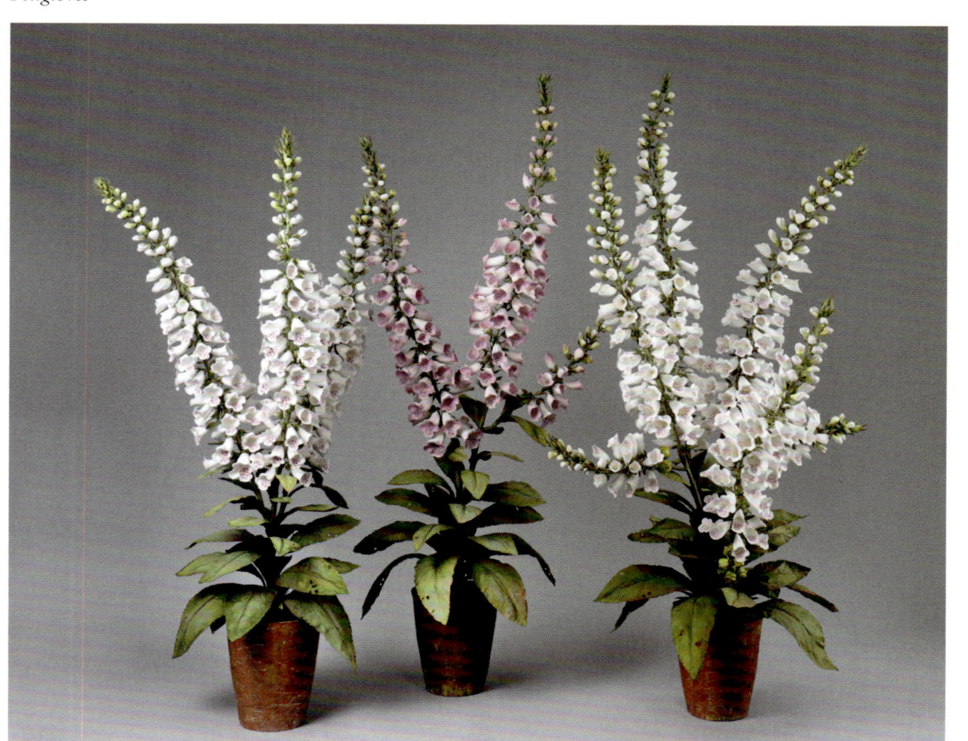

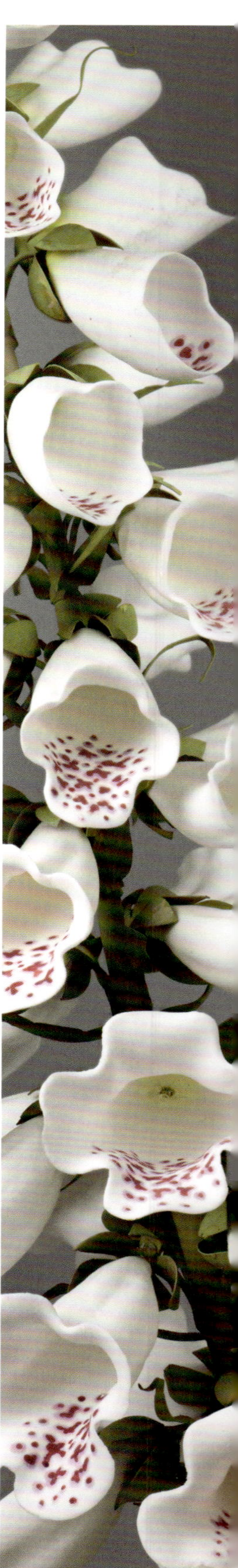

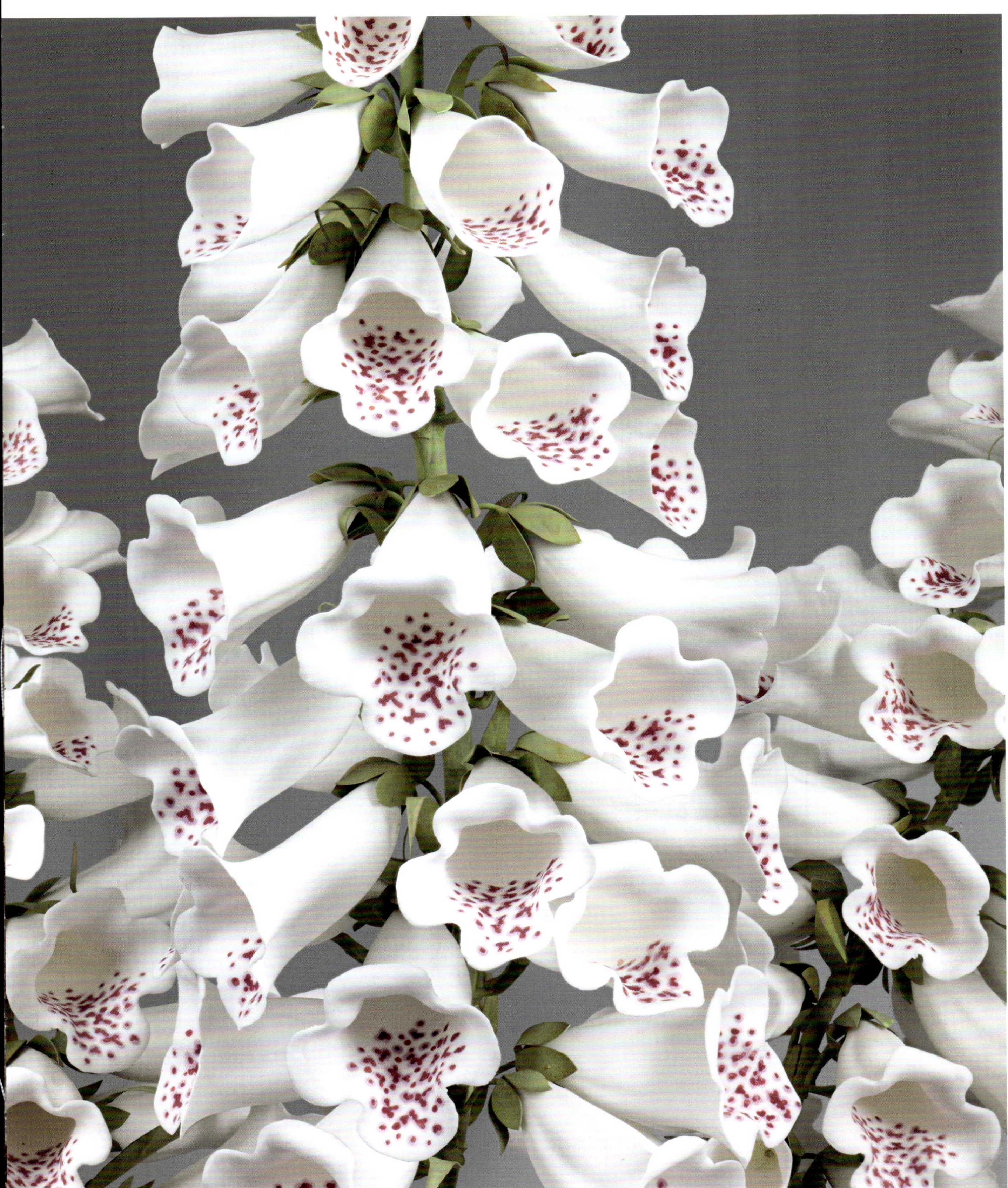

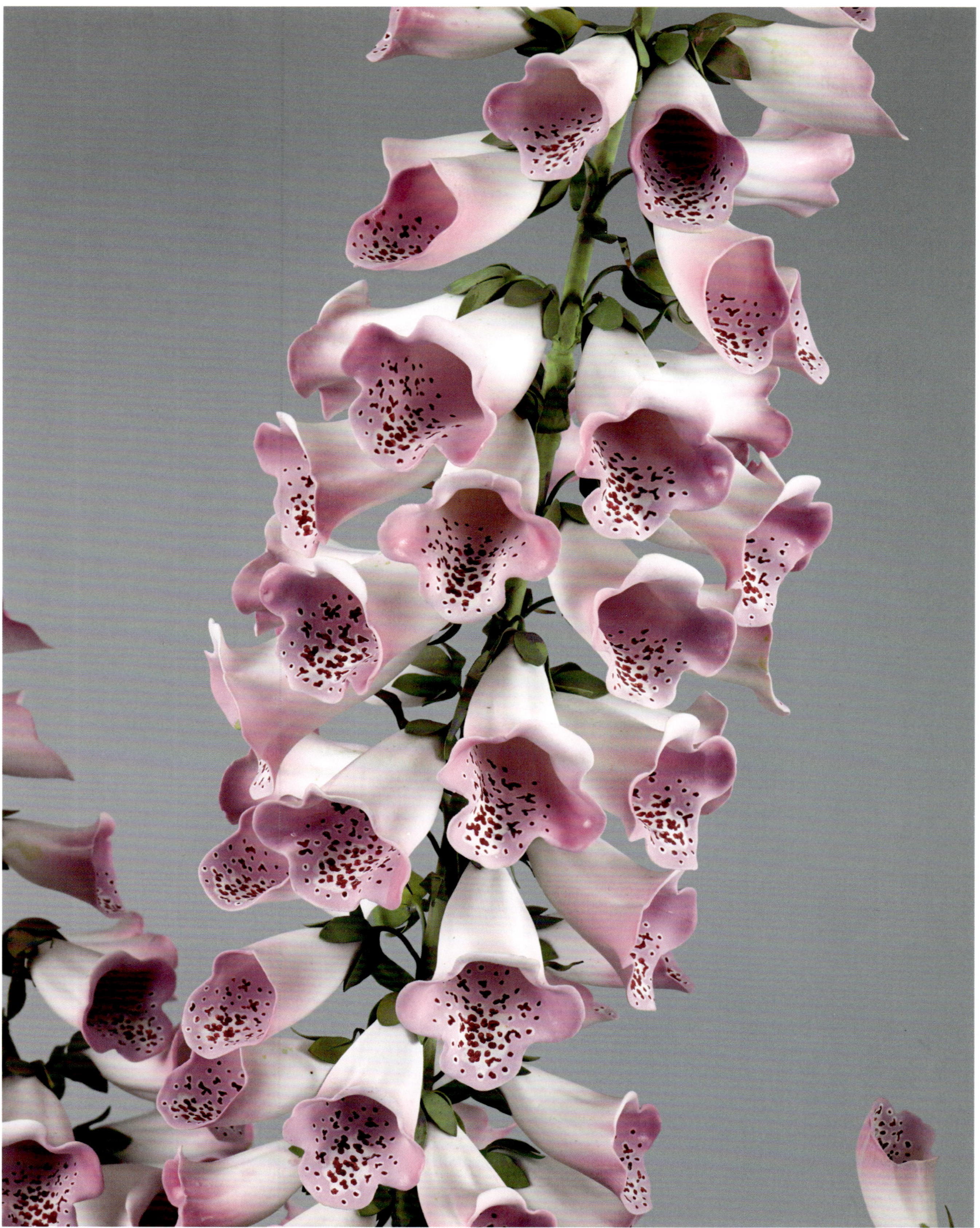

Foxgloves

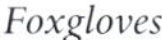

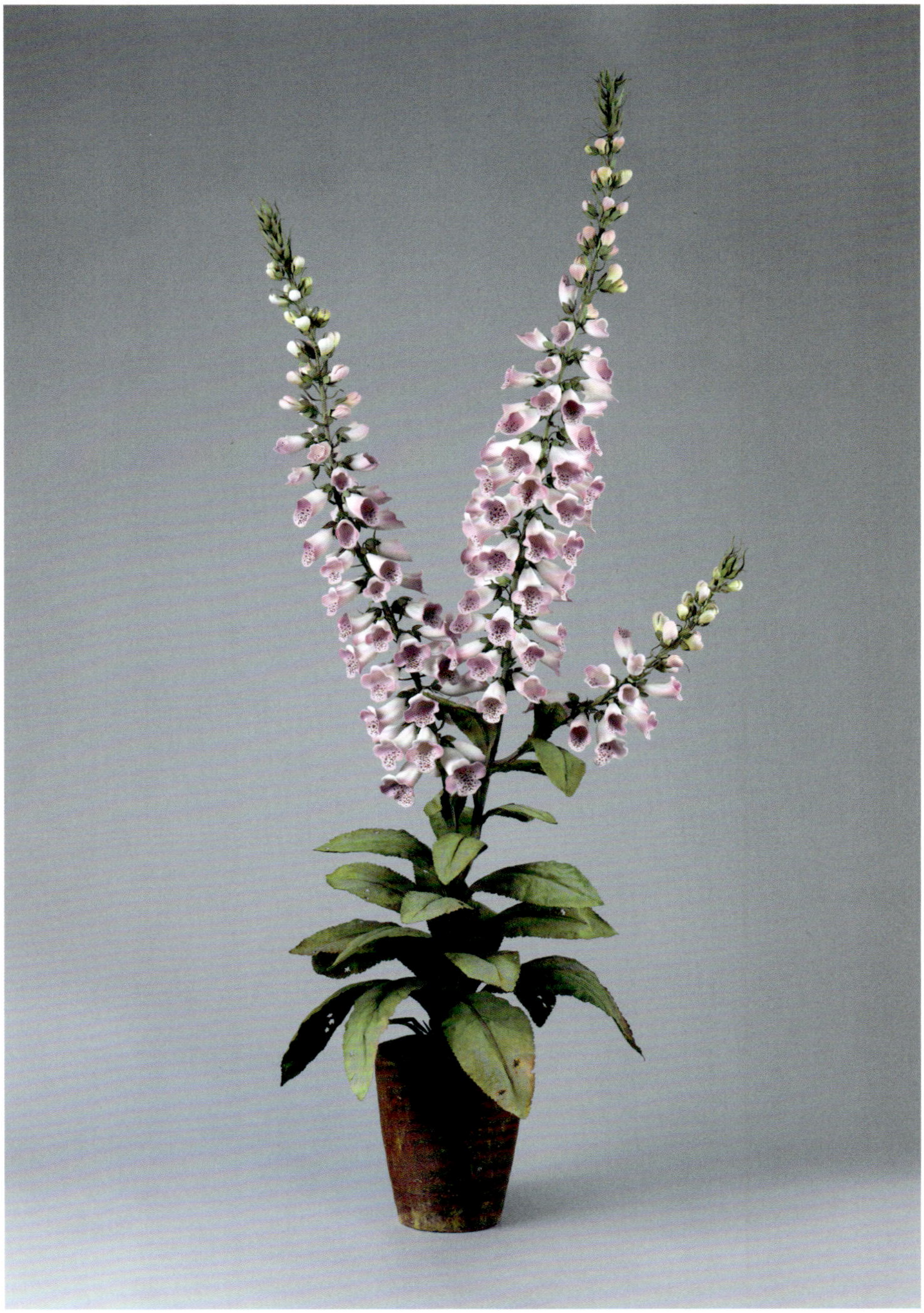

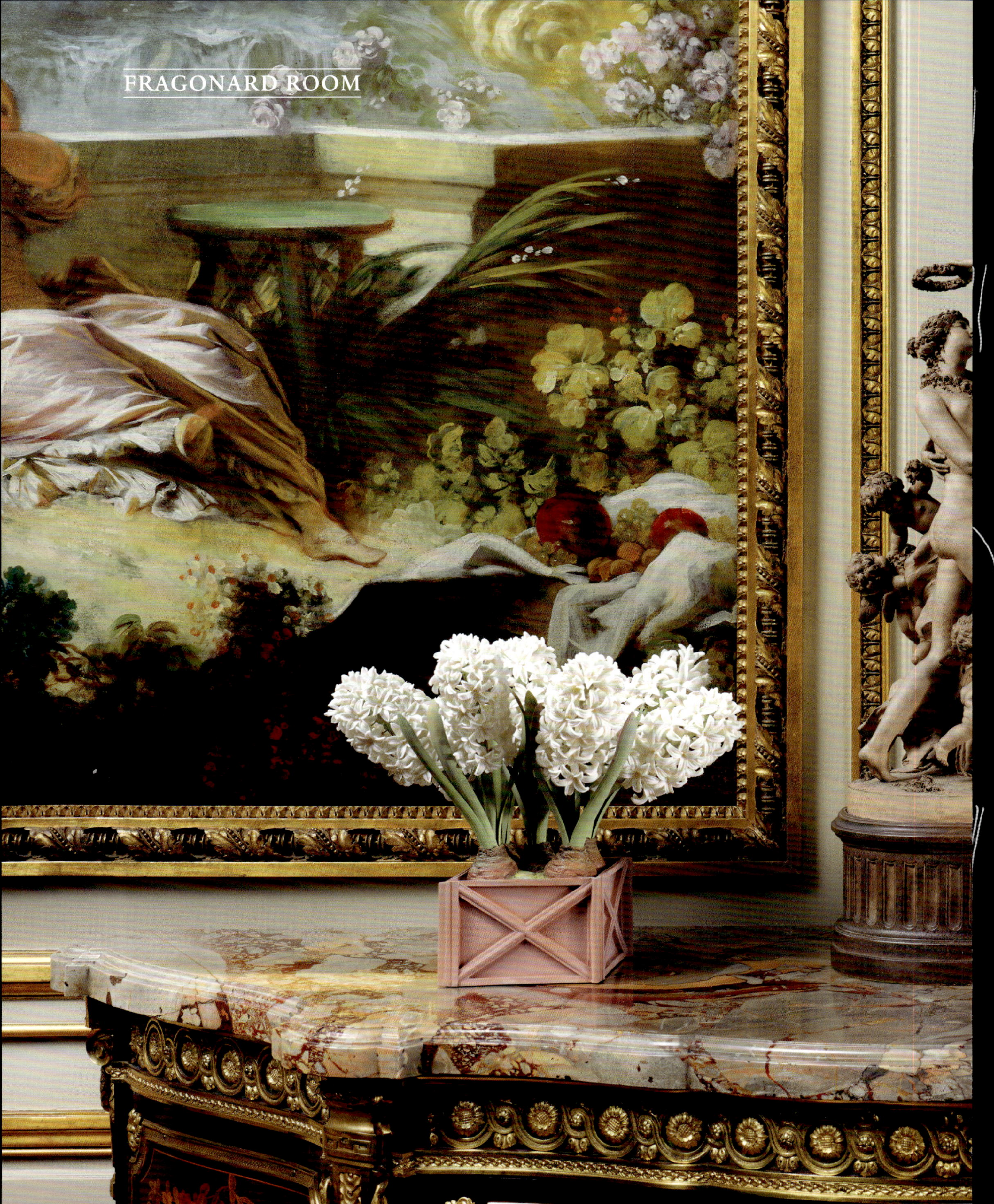
FRAGONARD ROOM

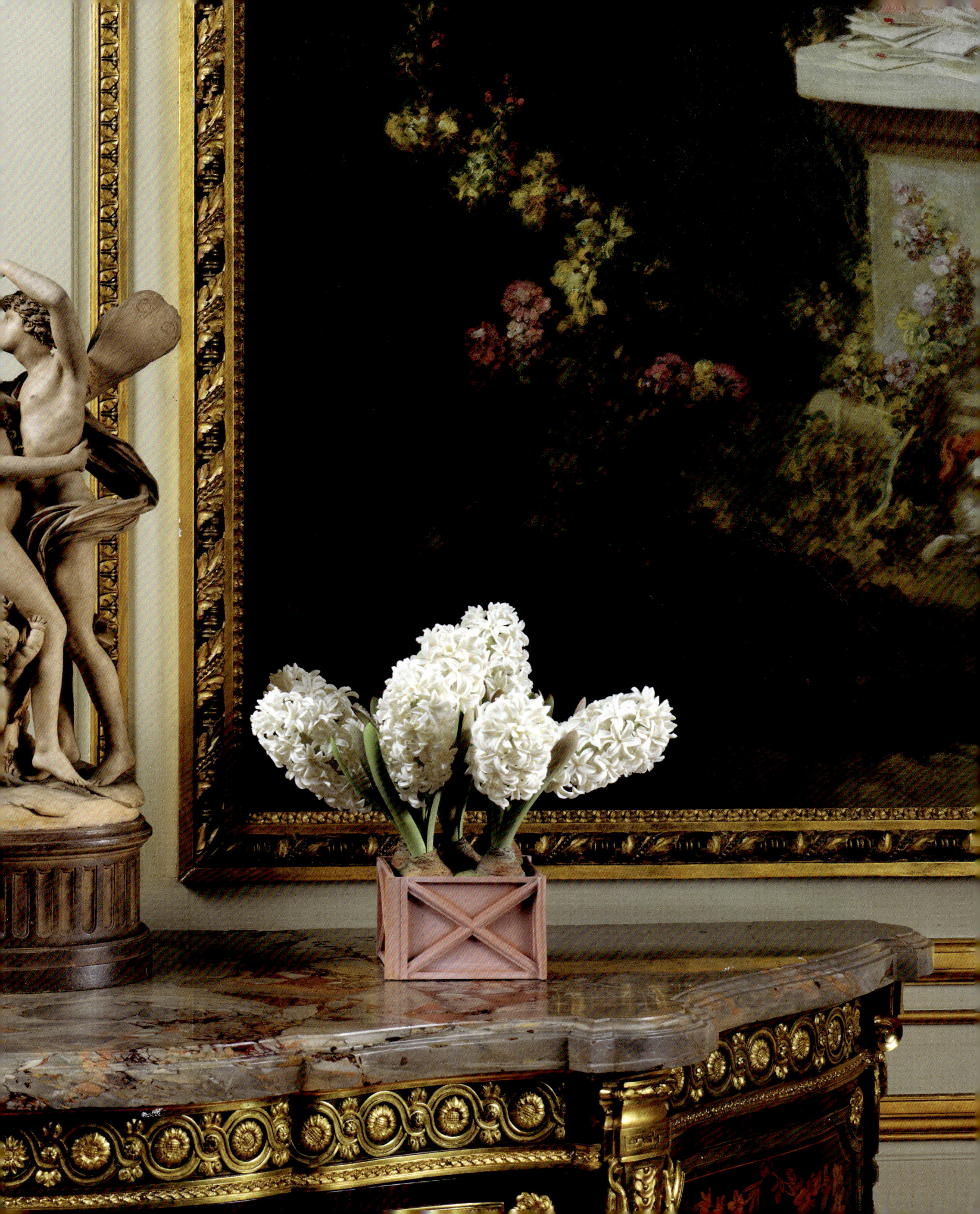

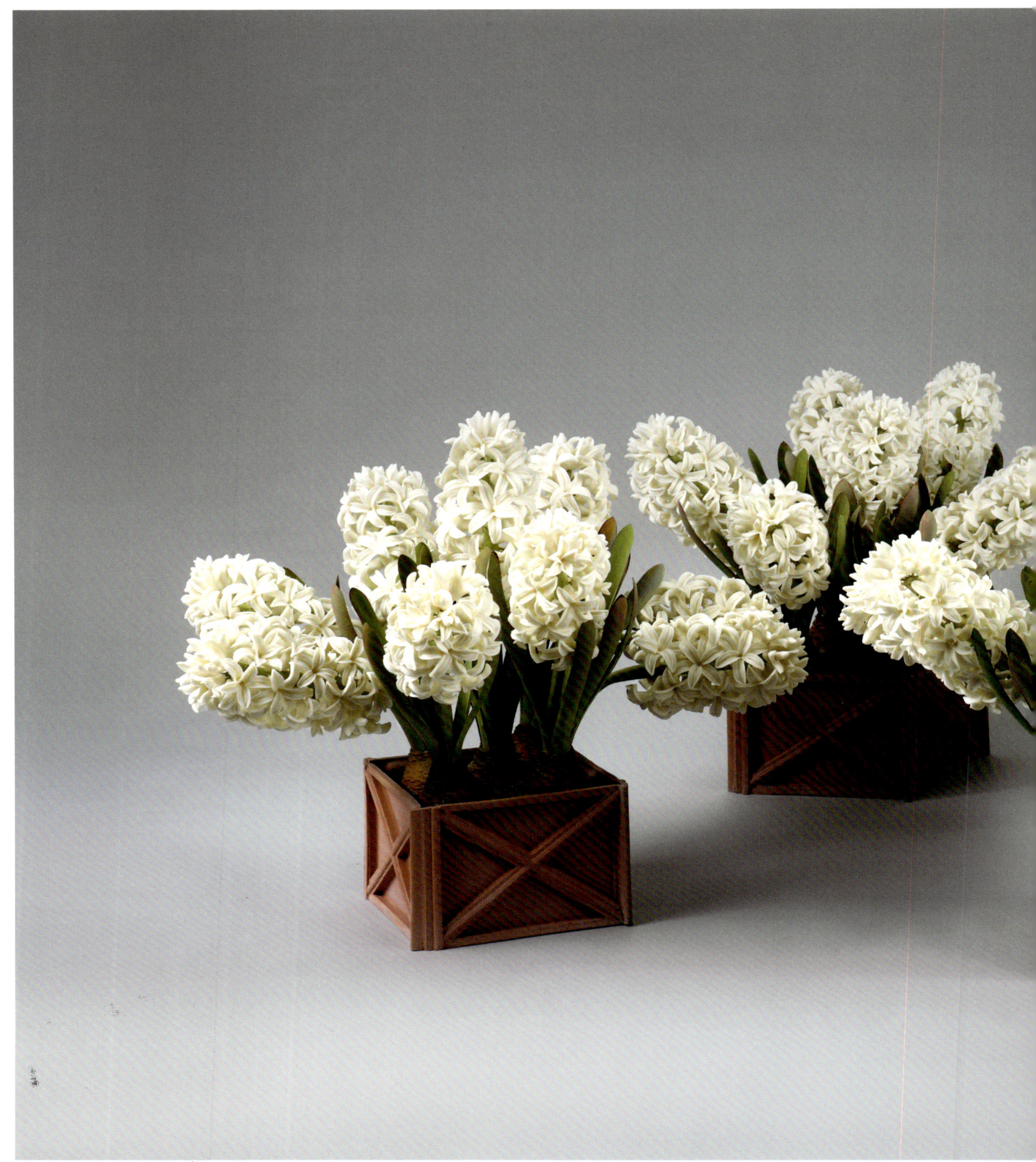

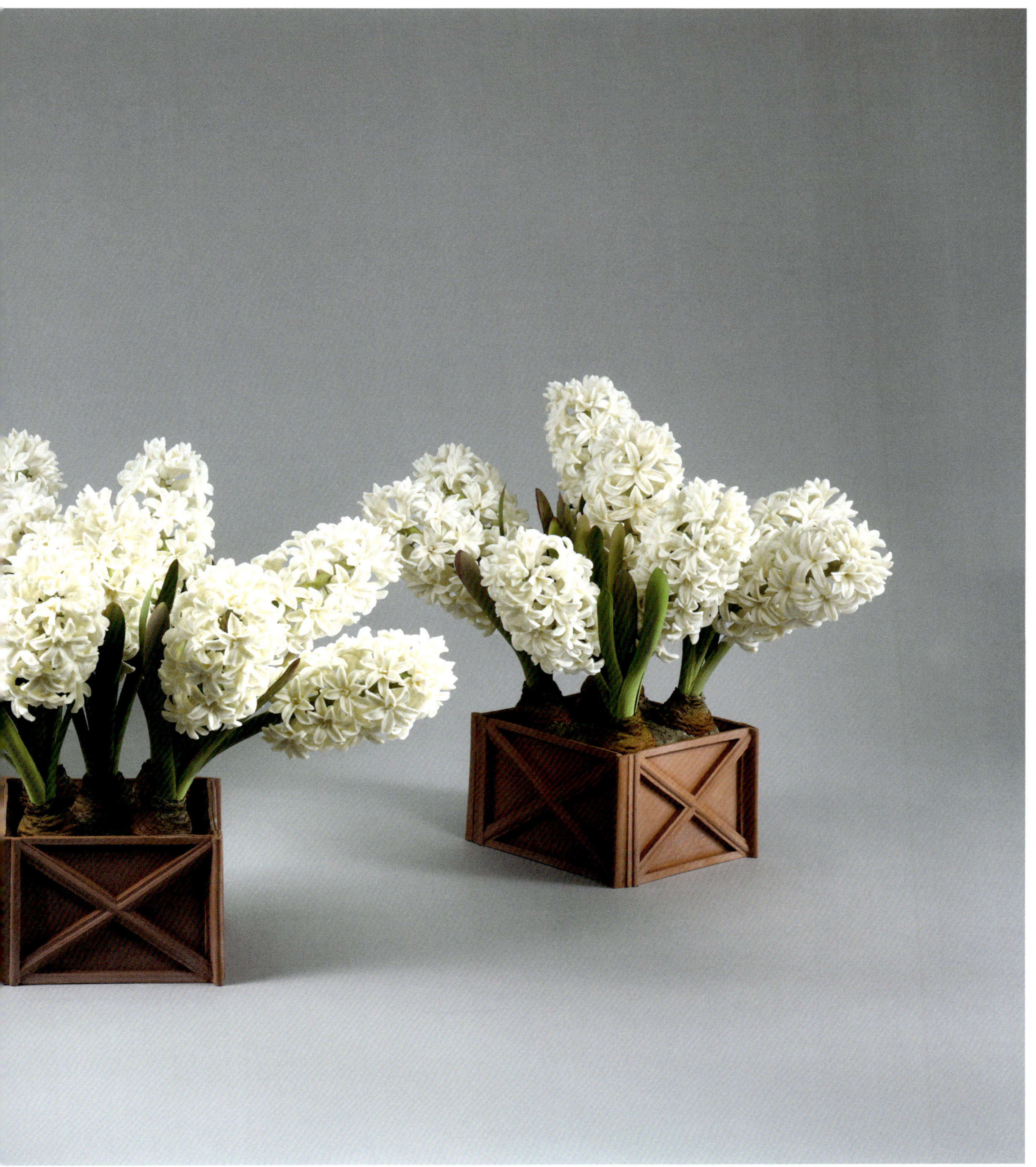

PREVIOUS PAGE
Hyacinths

Roses

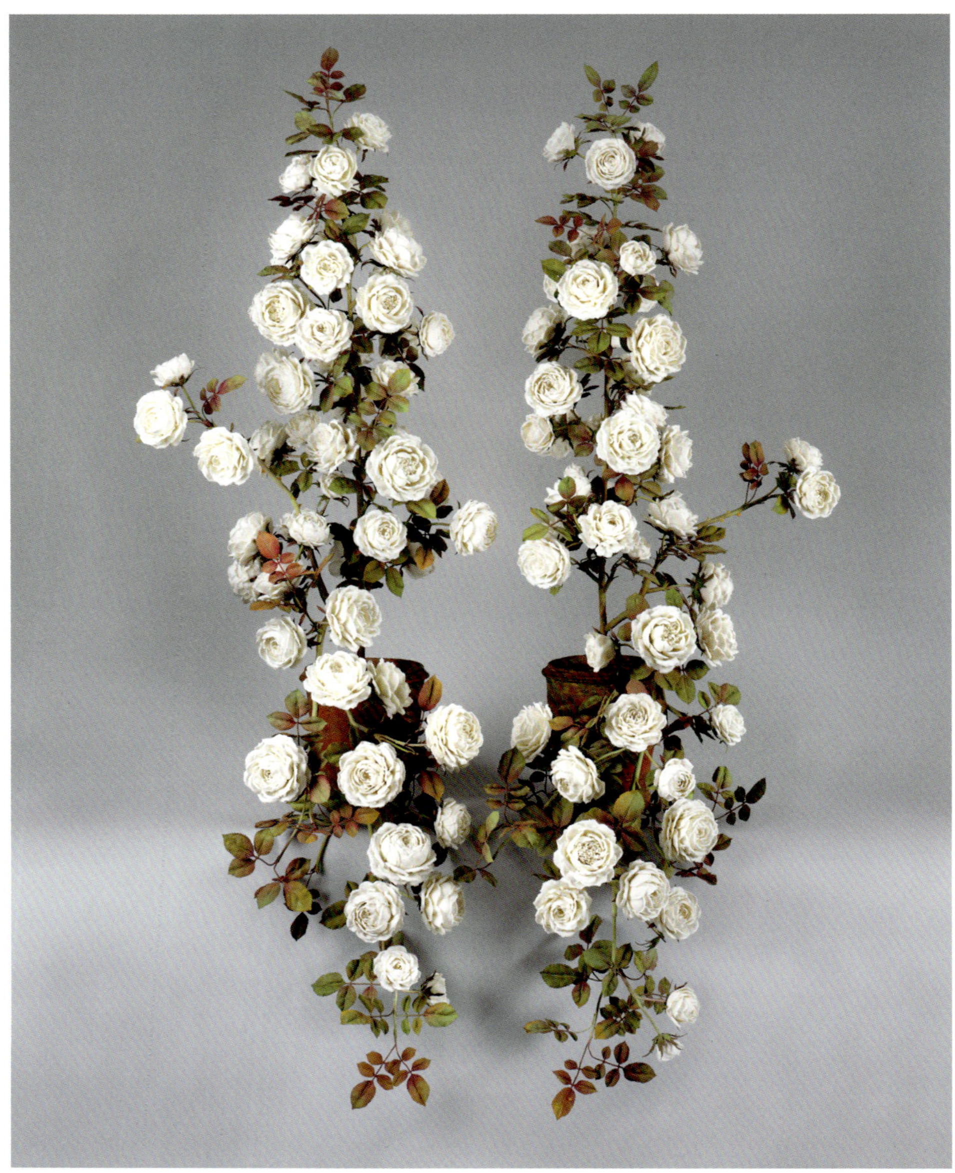

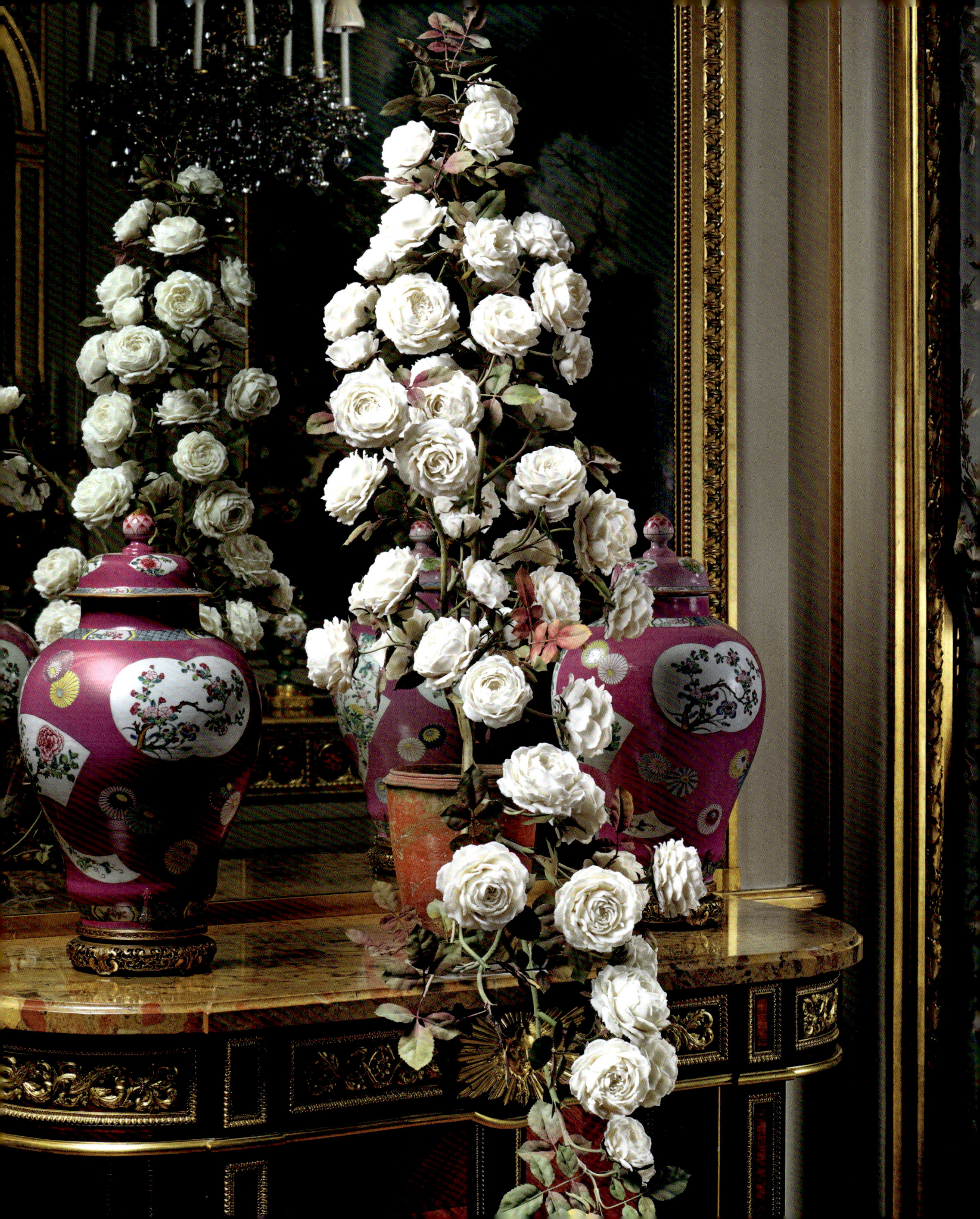

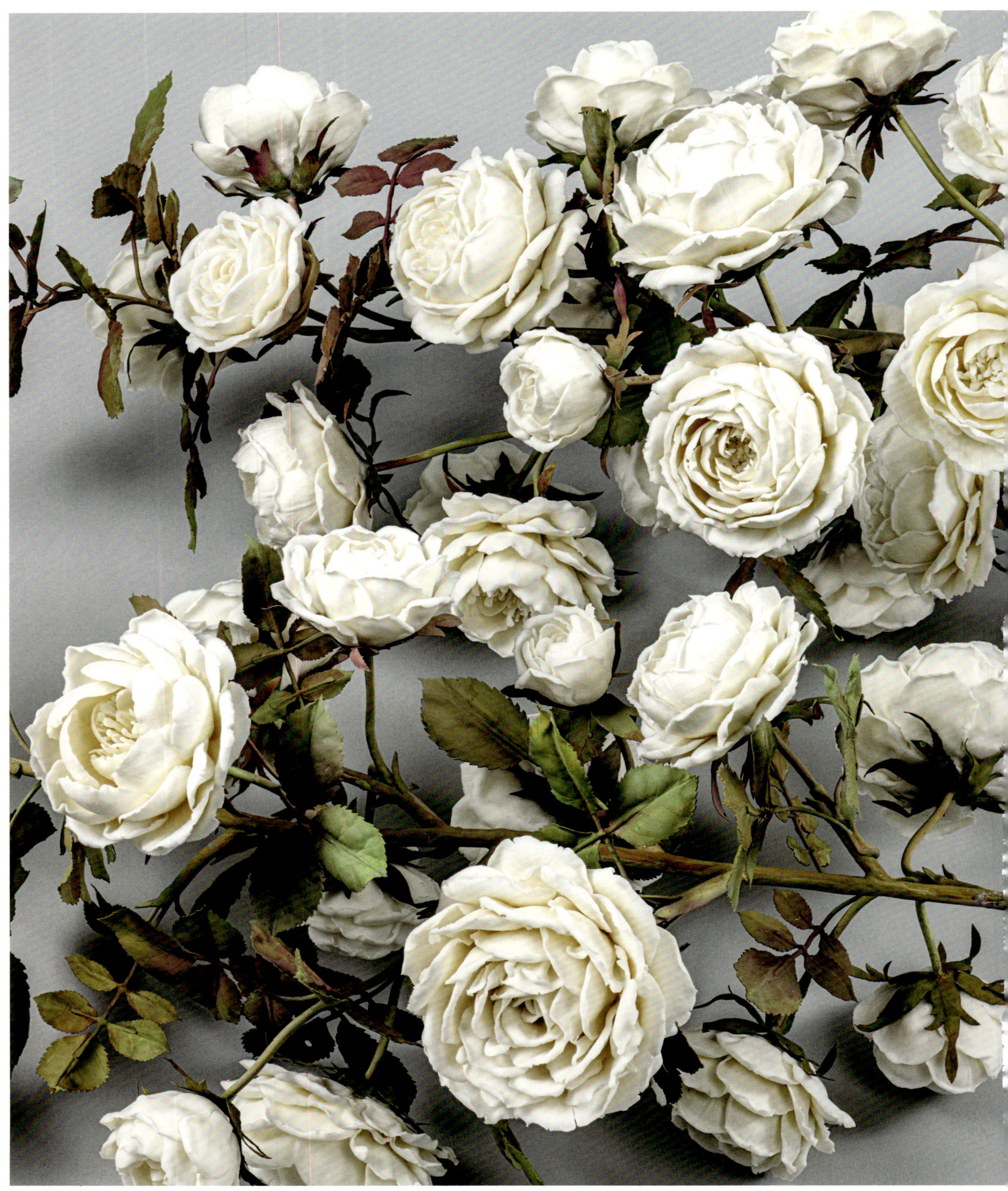

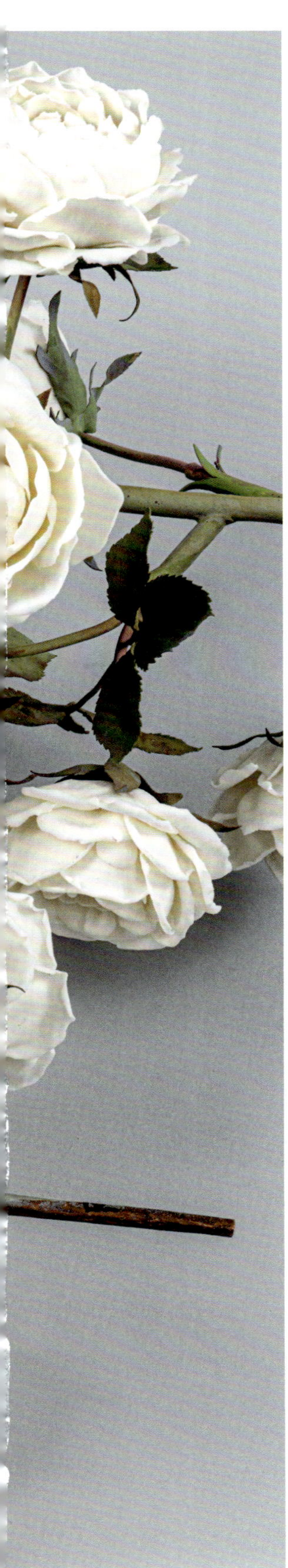

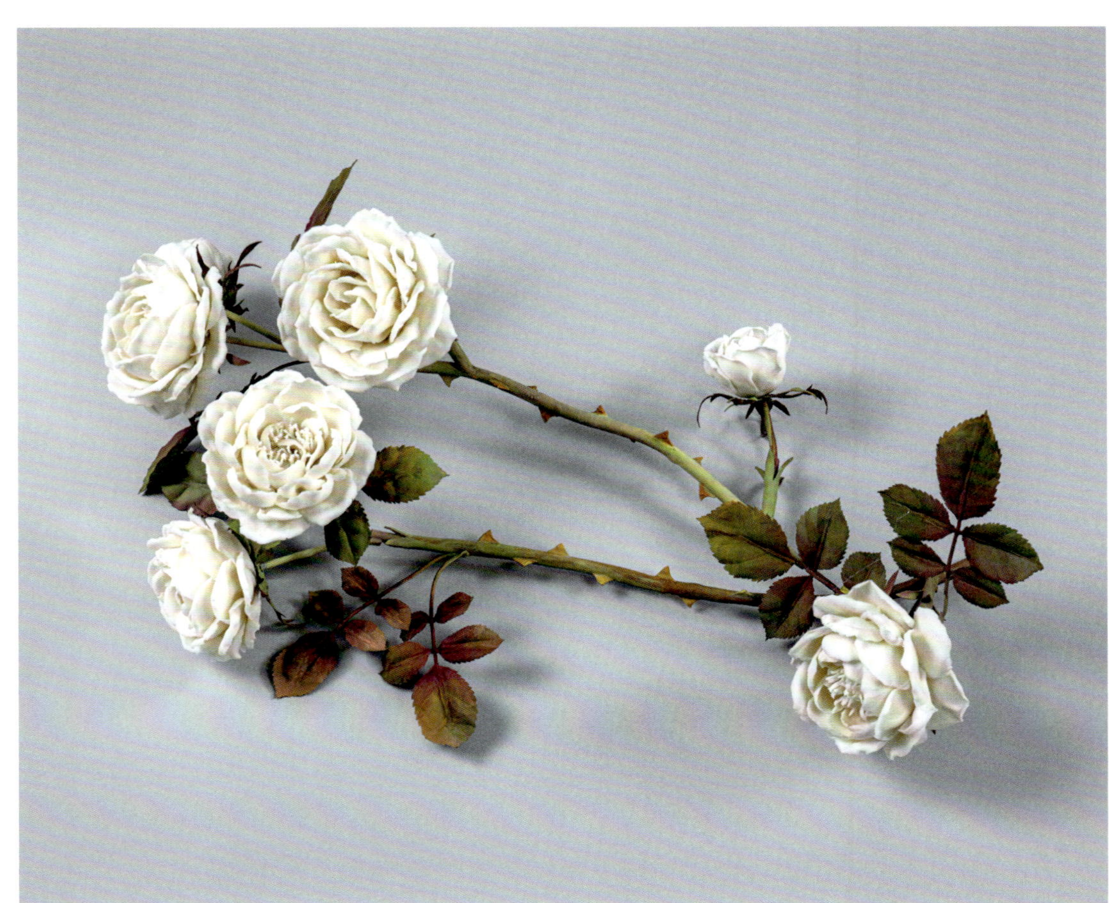

Roses

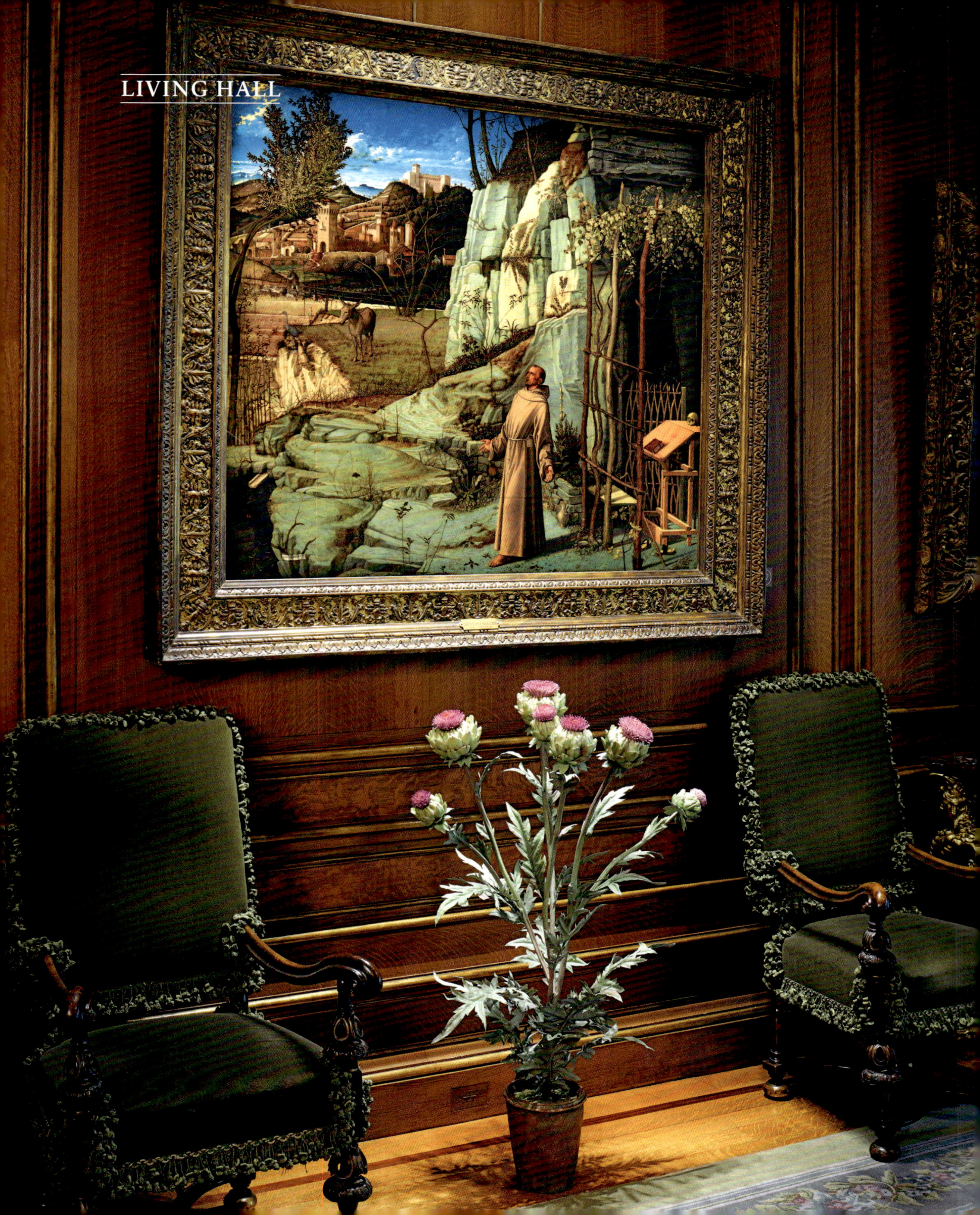

LIVING HALL

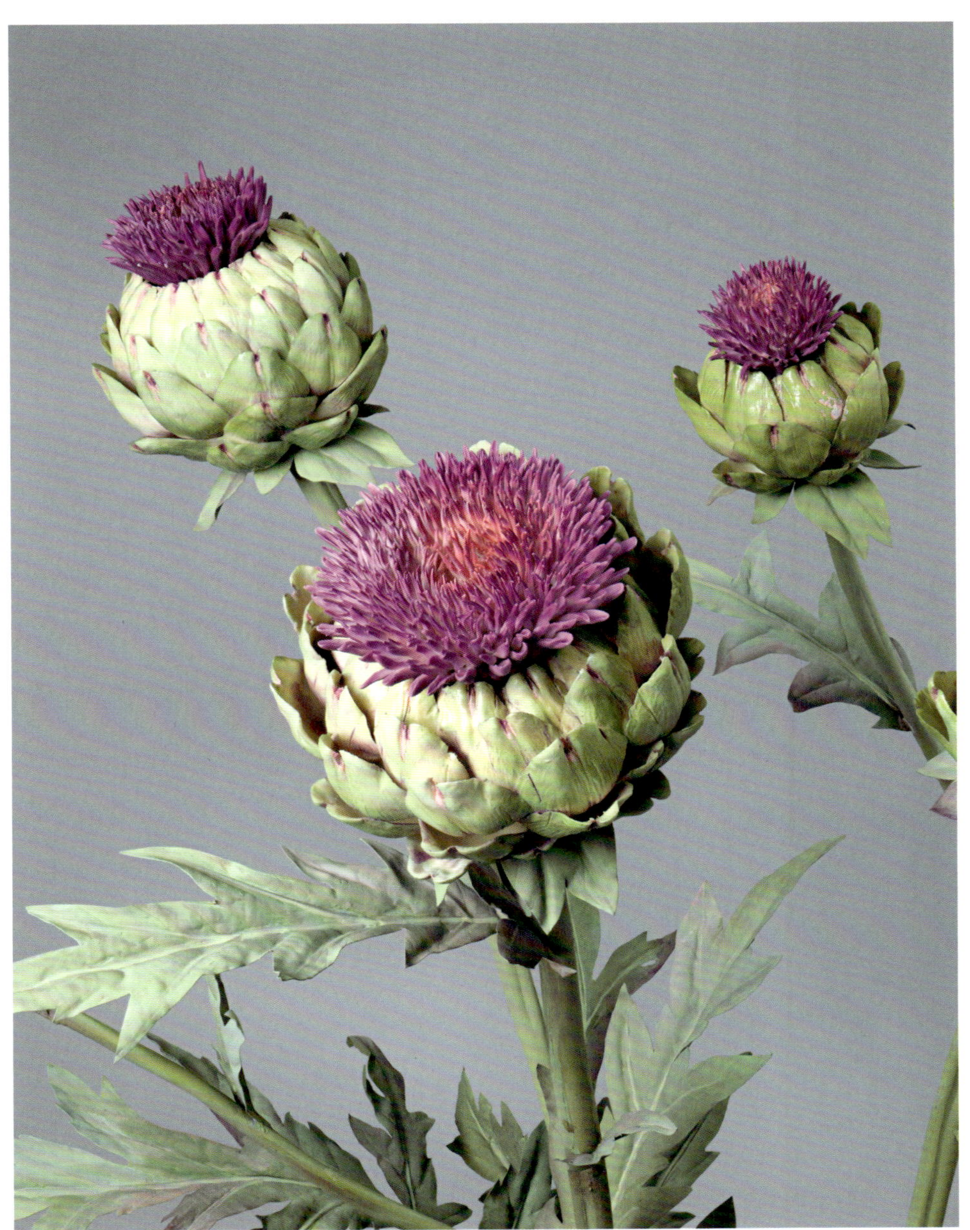

Artichoke plant

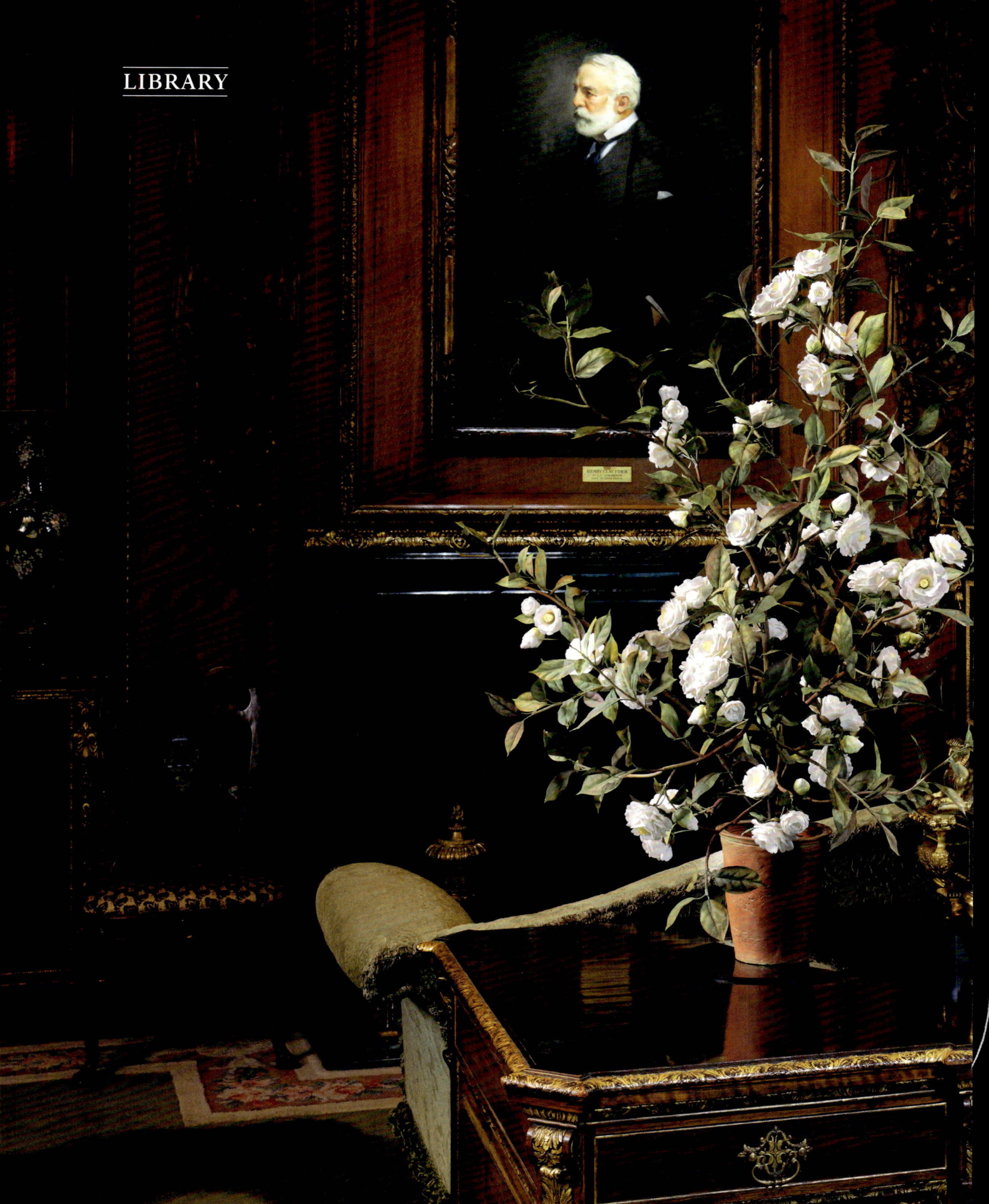

LIBRARY

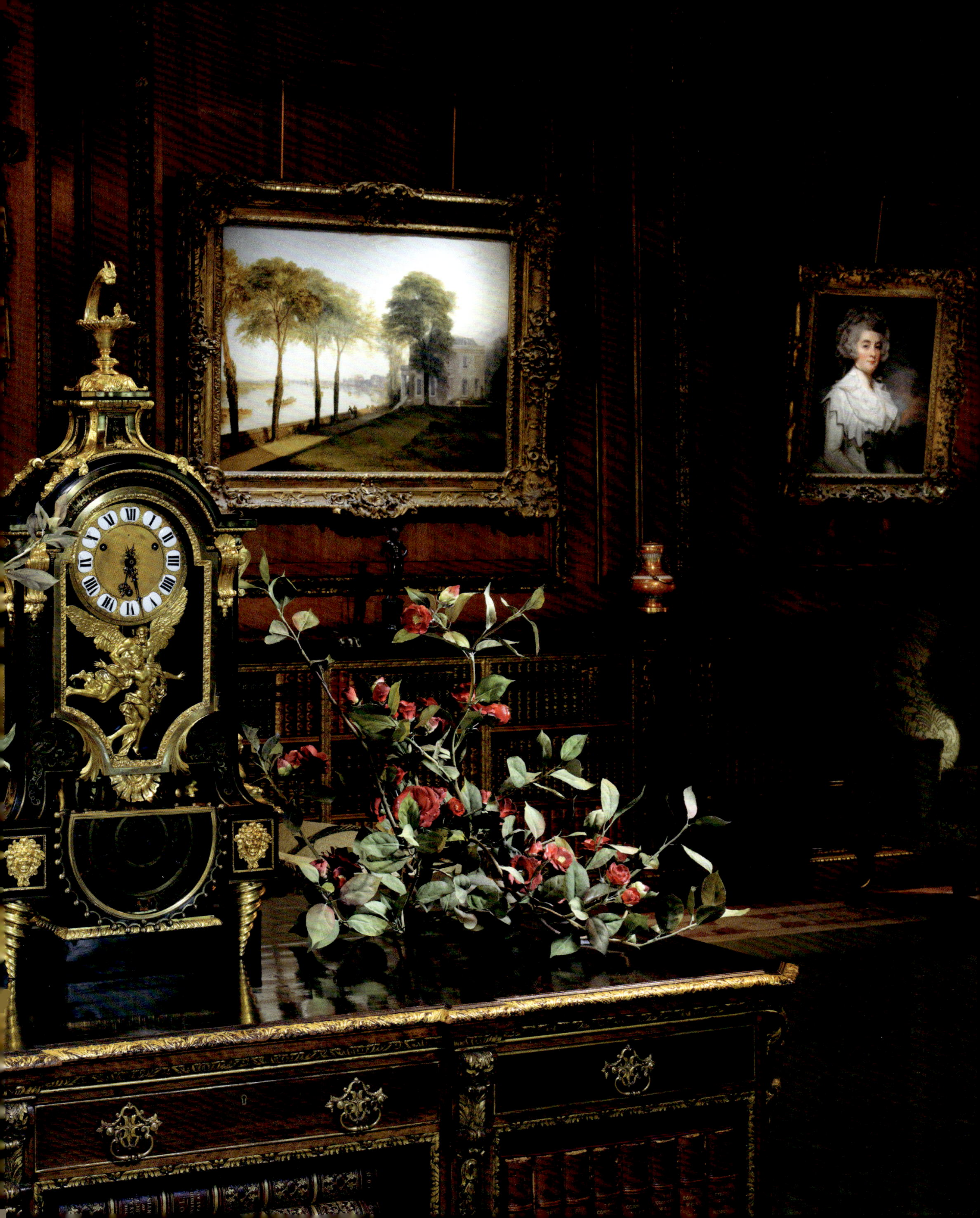

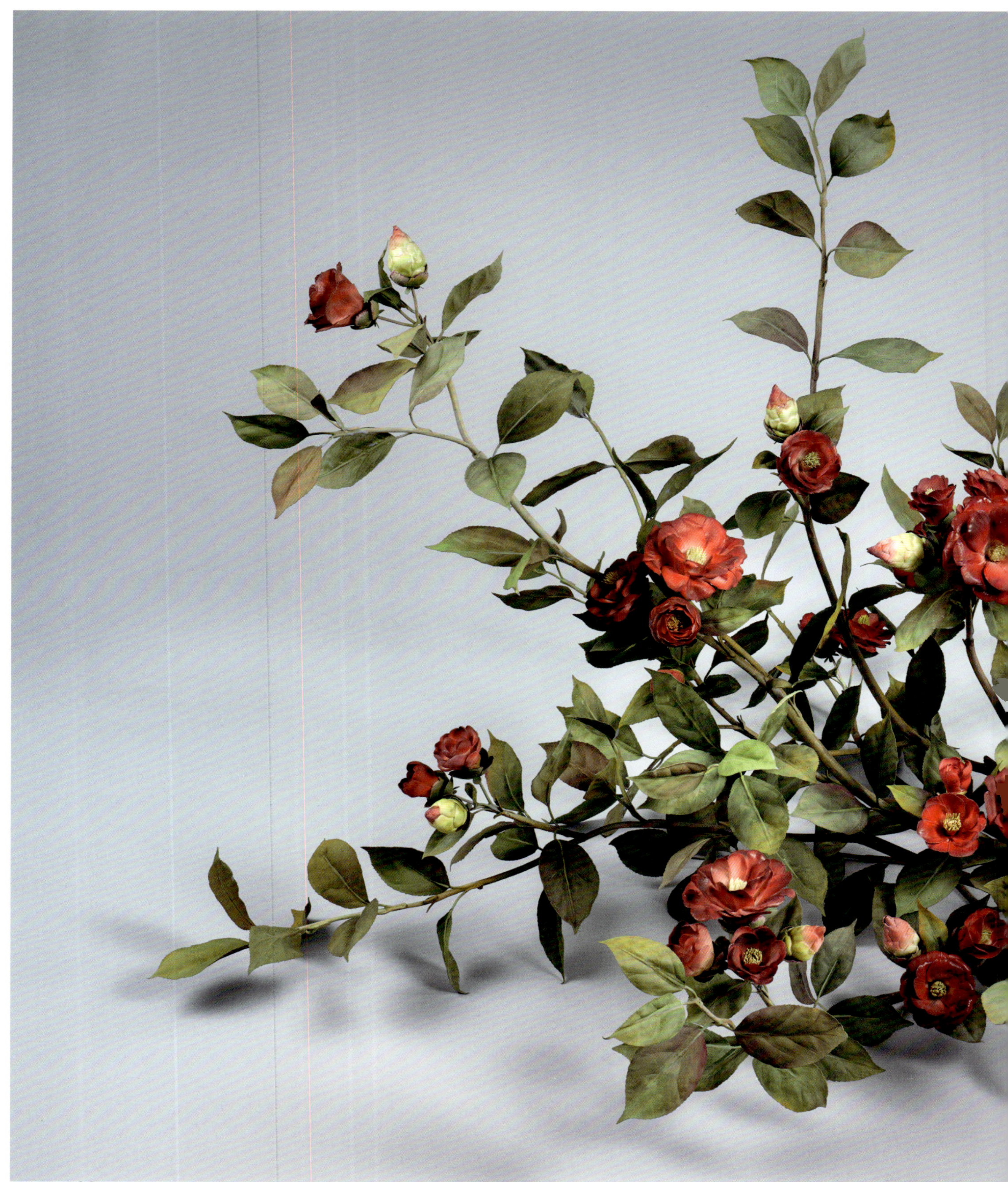

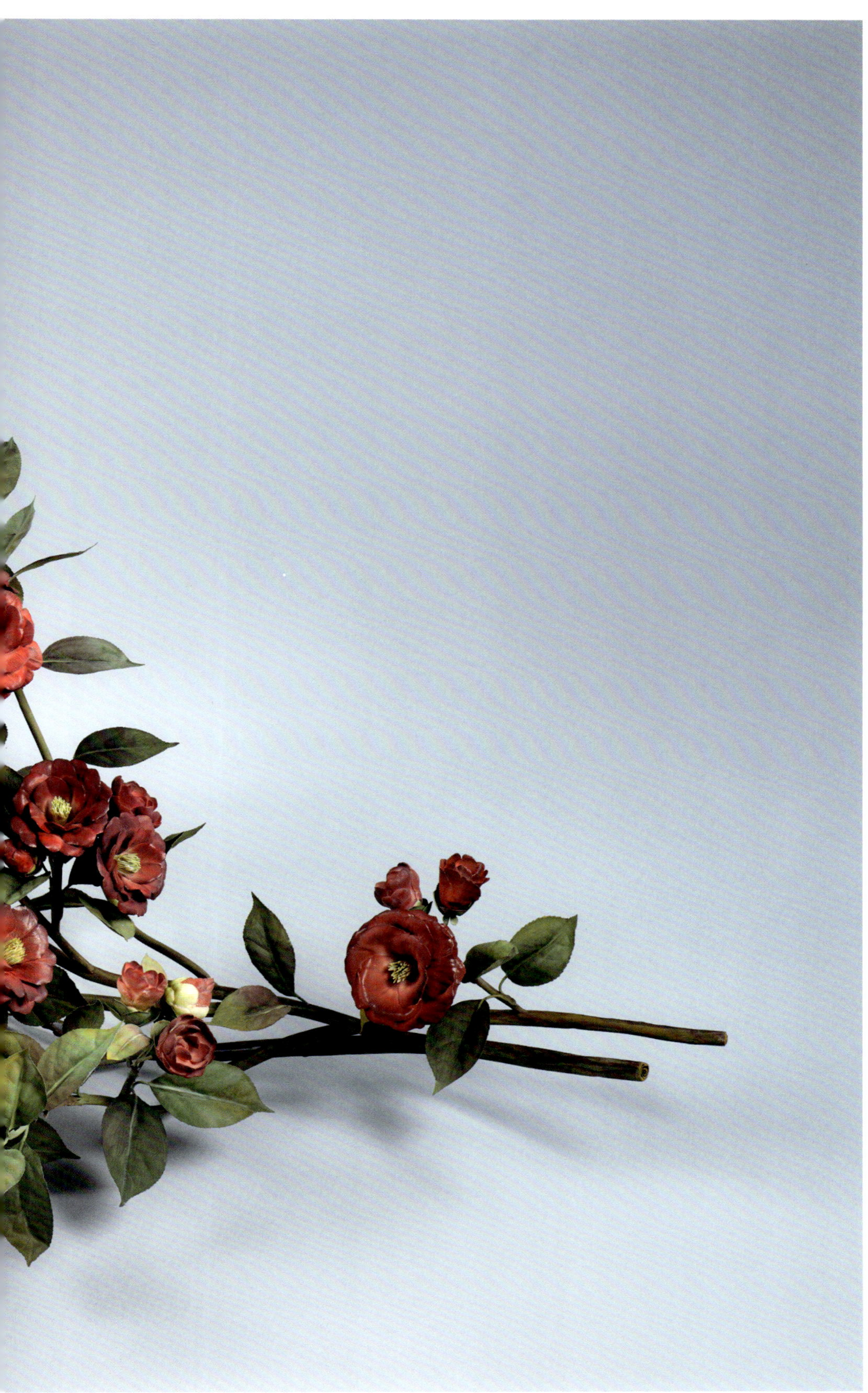

Camellia branches

39

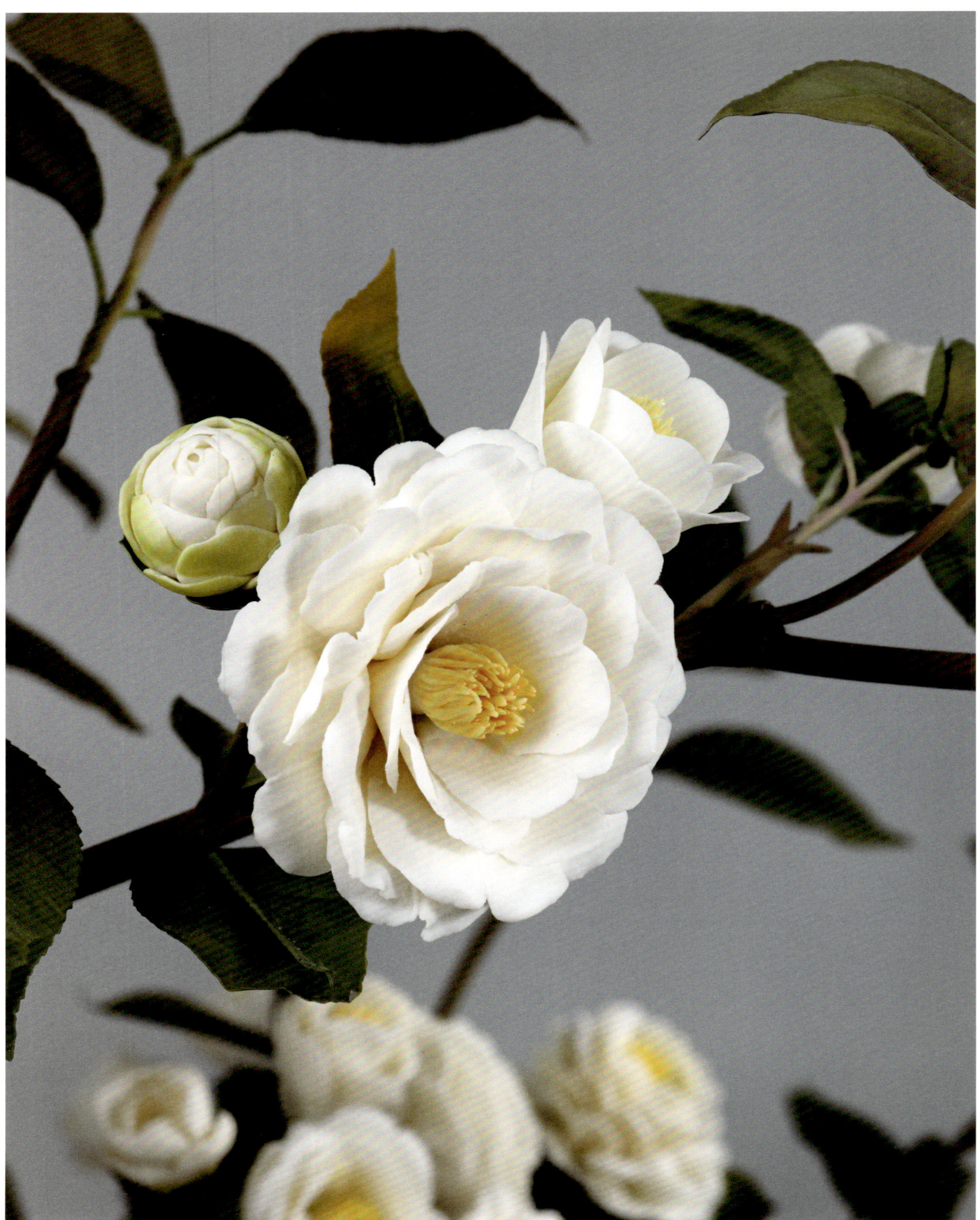

Camellia plant

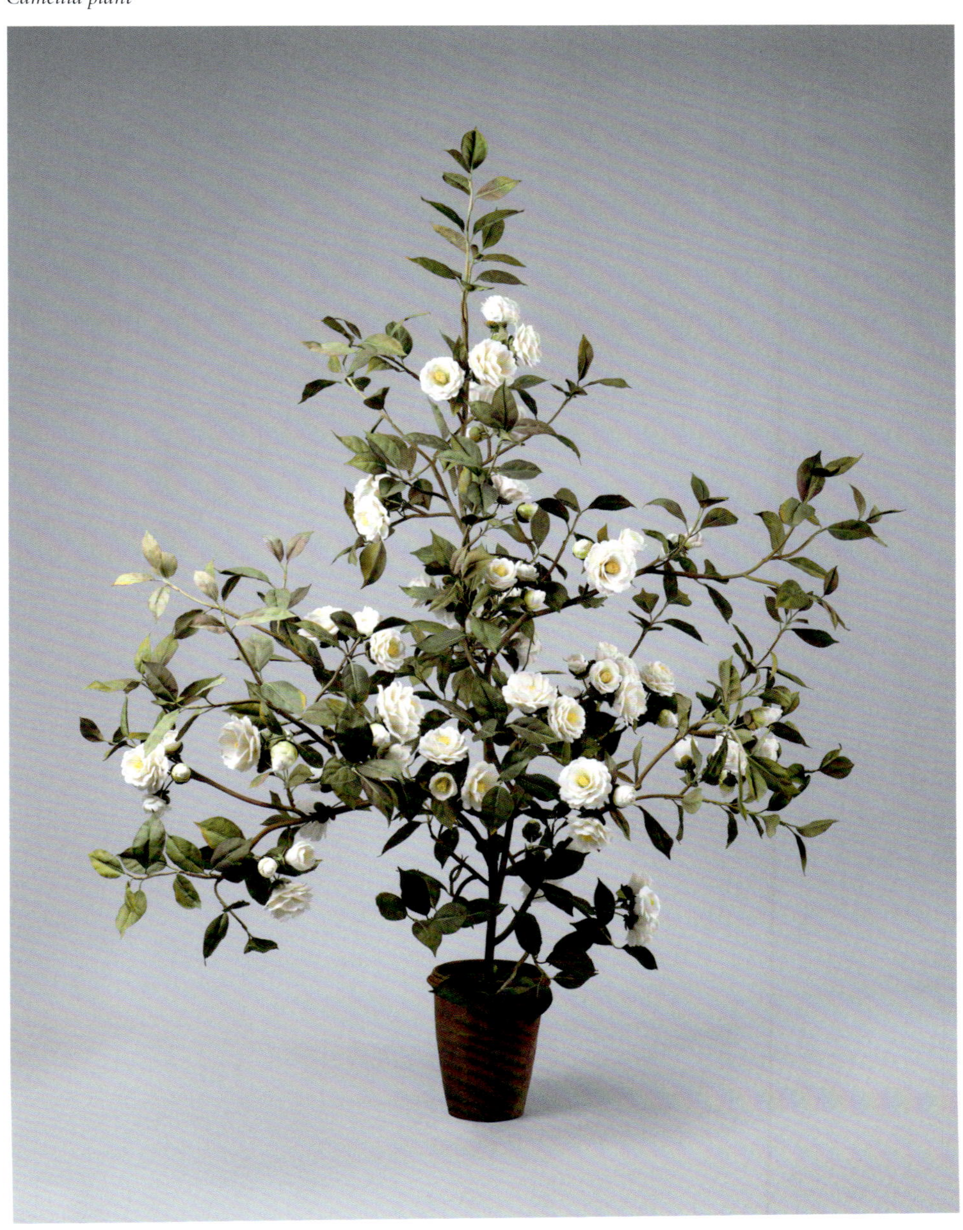

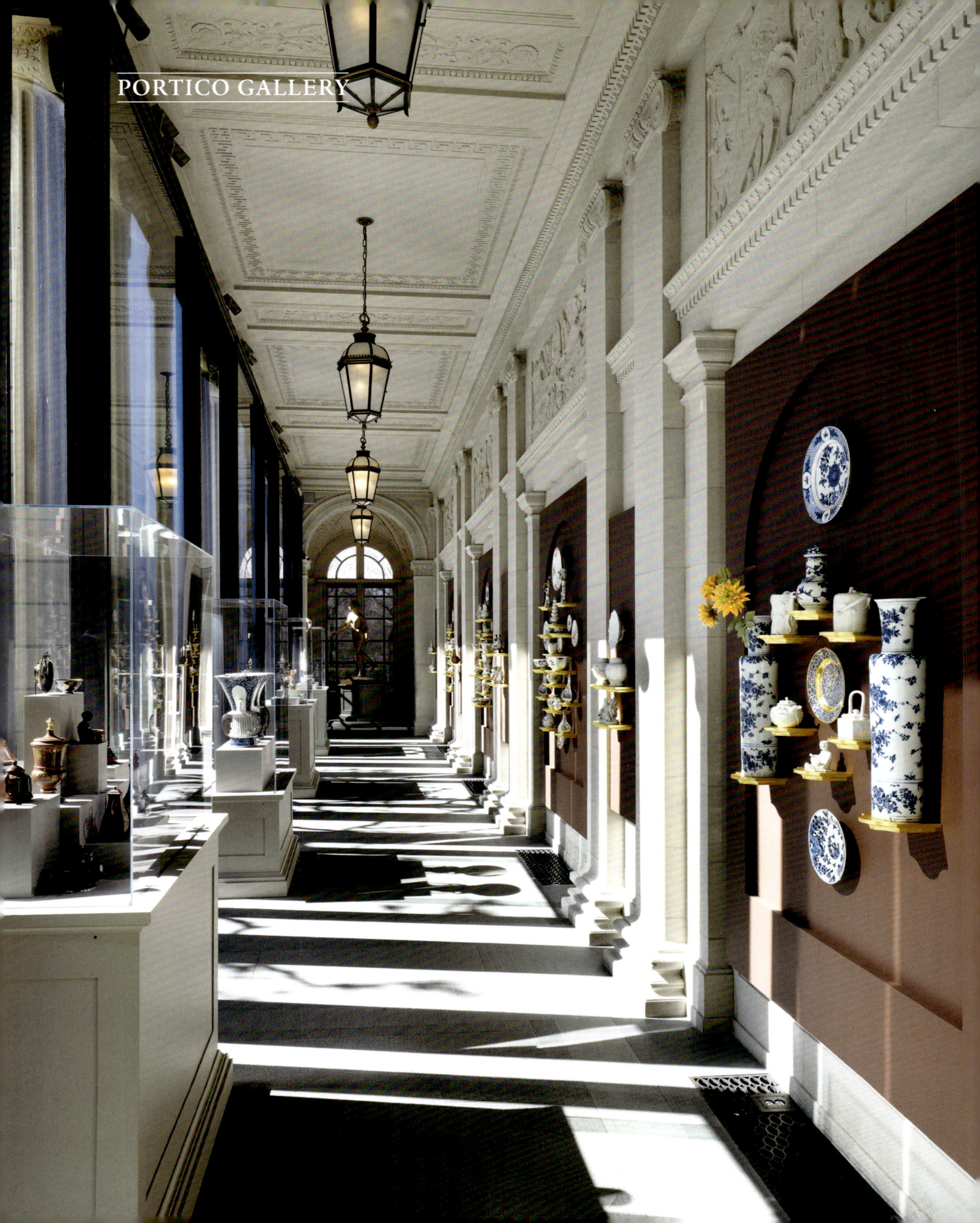
PORTICO GALLERY

Dahlia branch

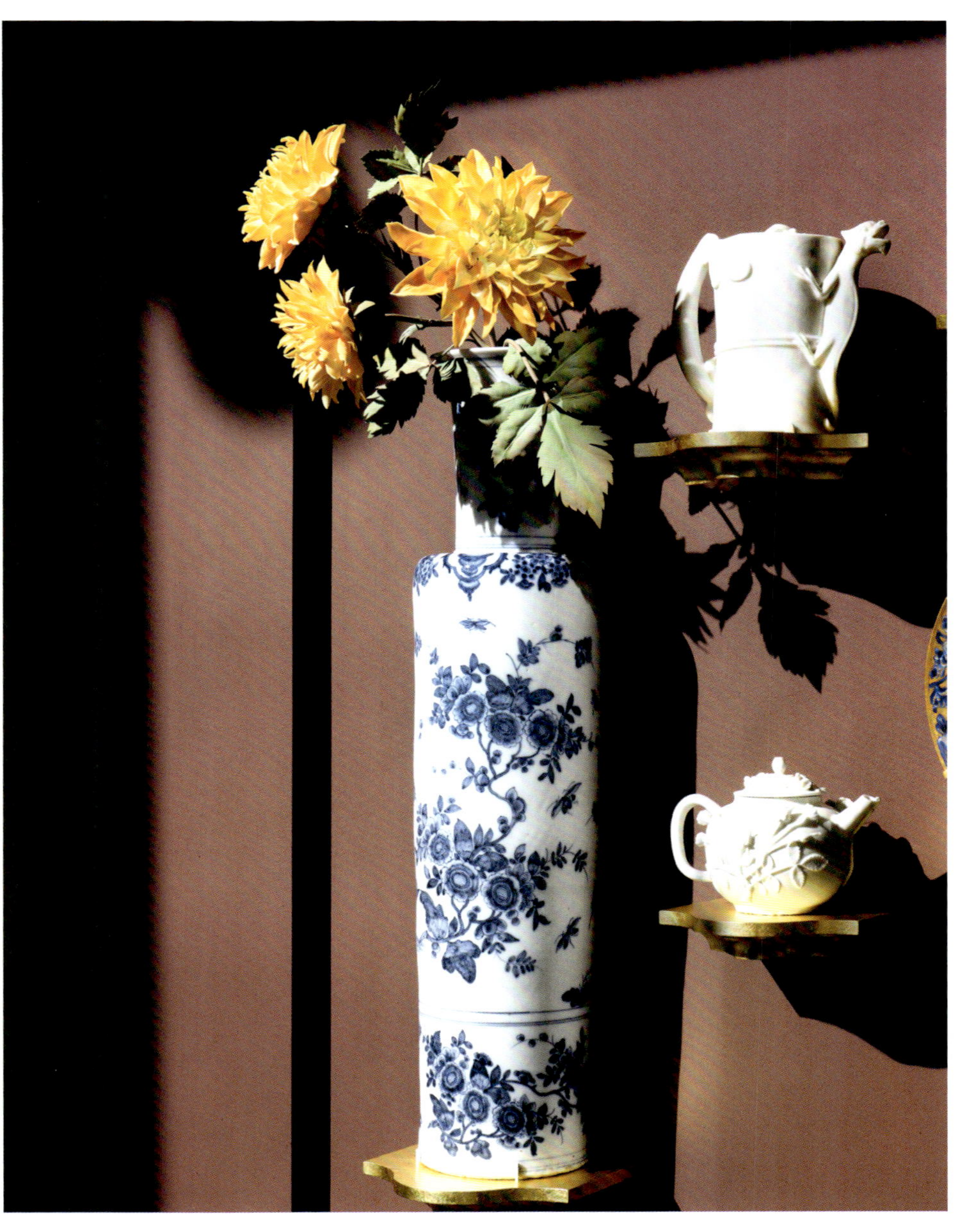

Anemones

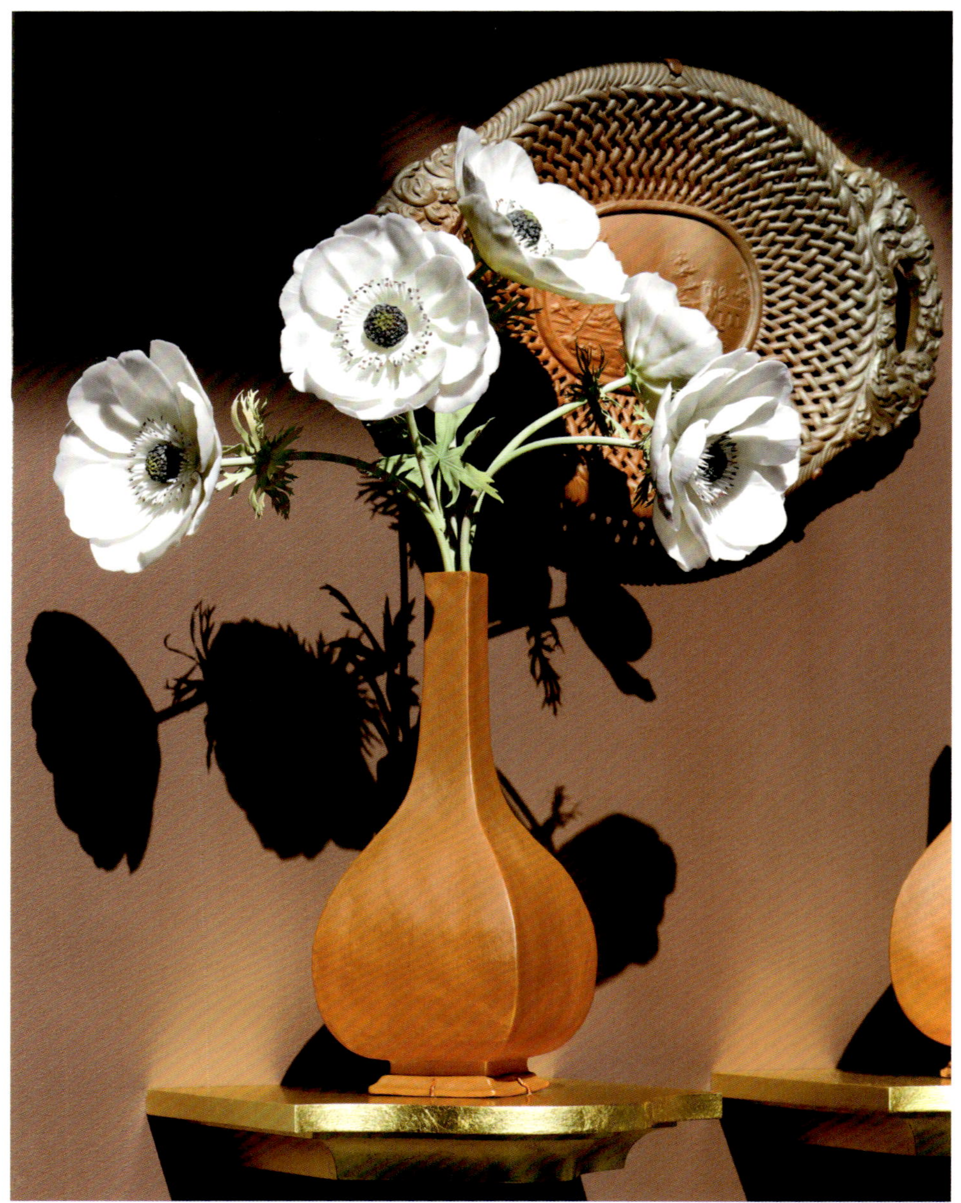

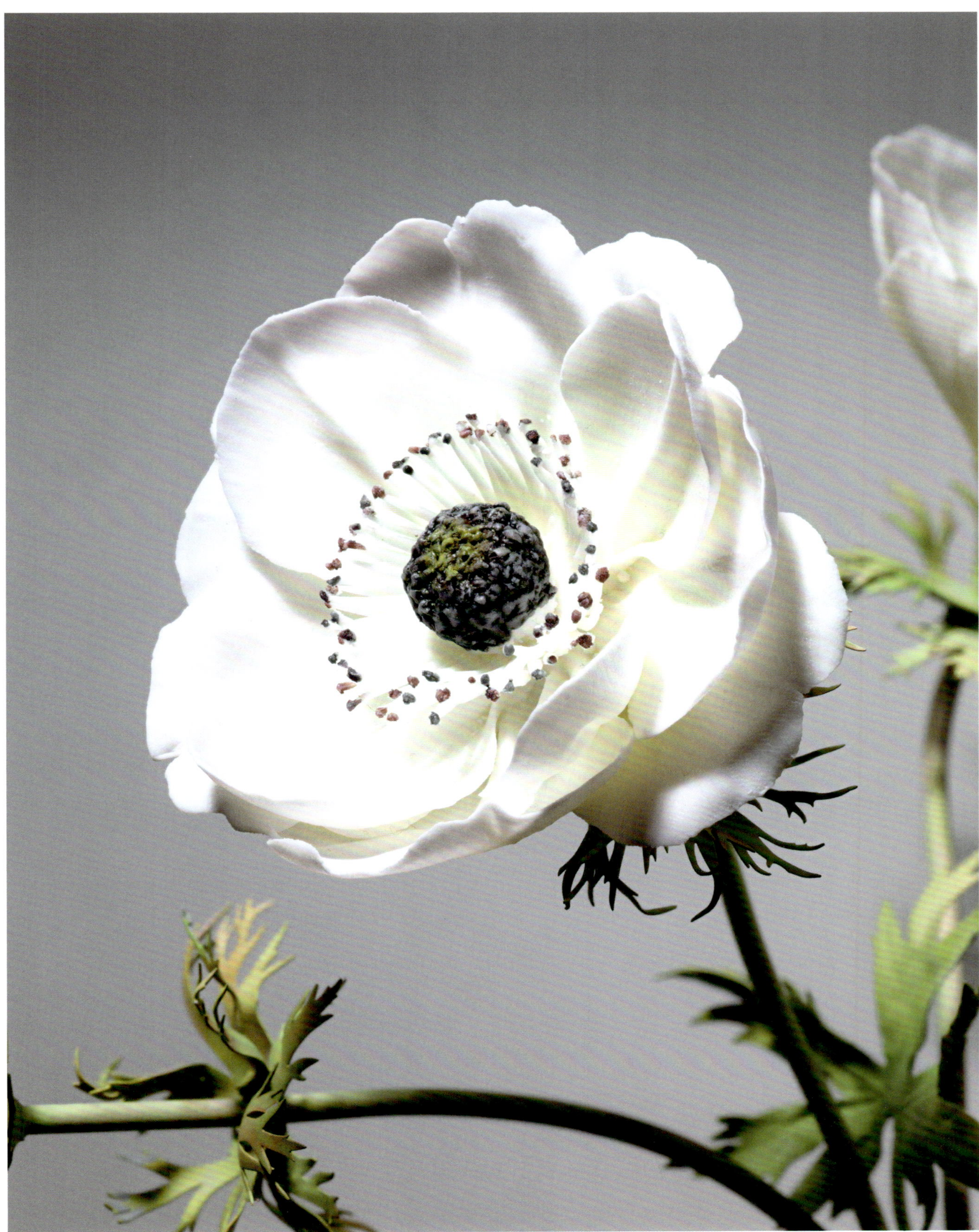

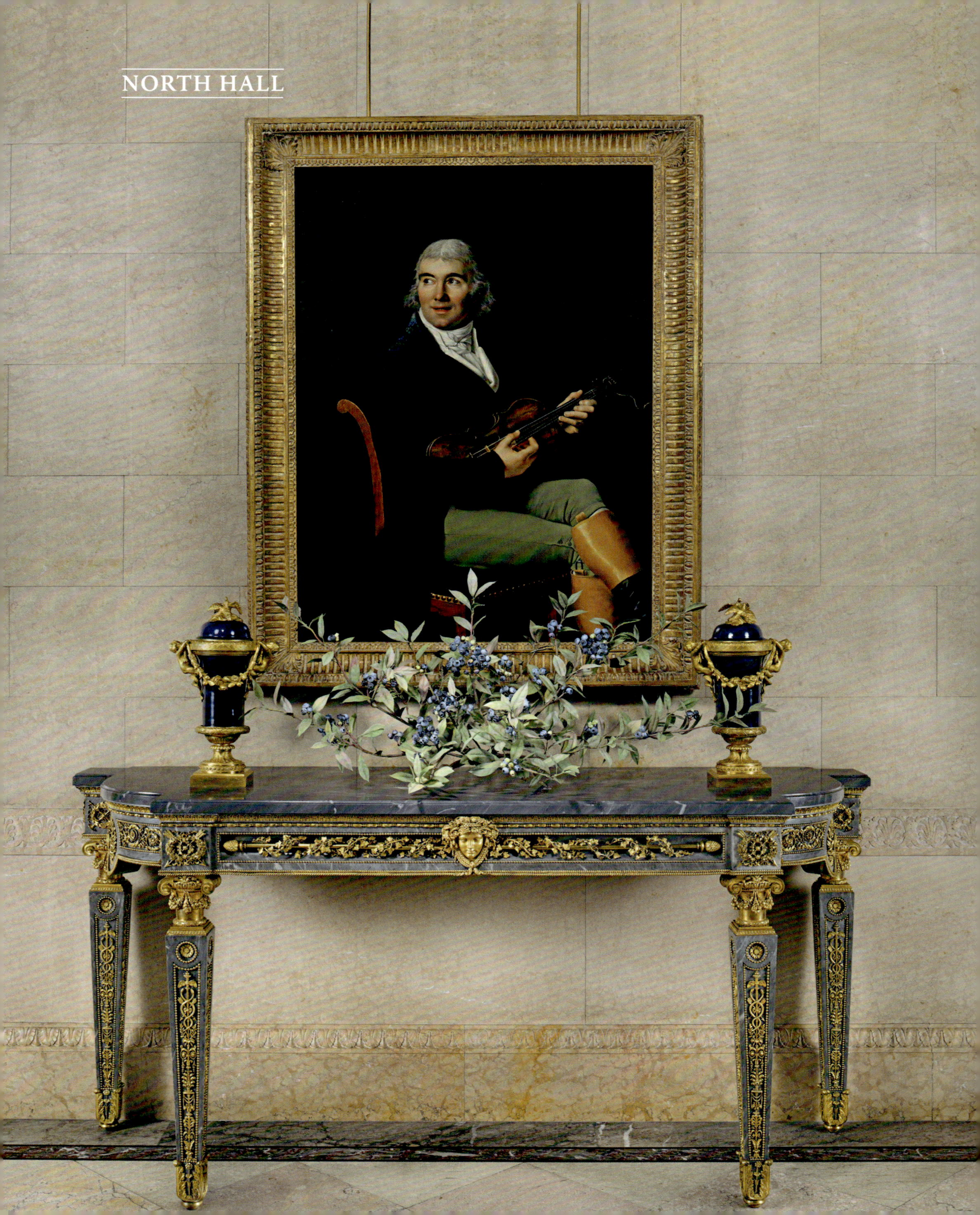

Blueberry branches

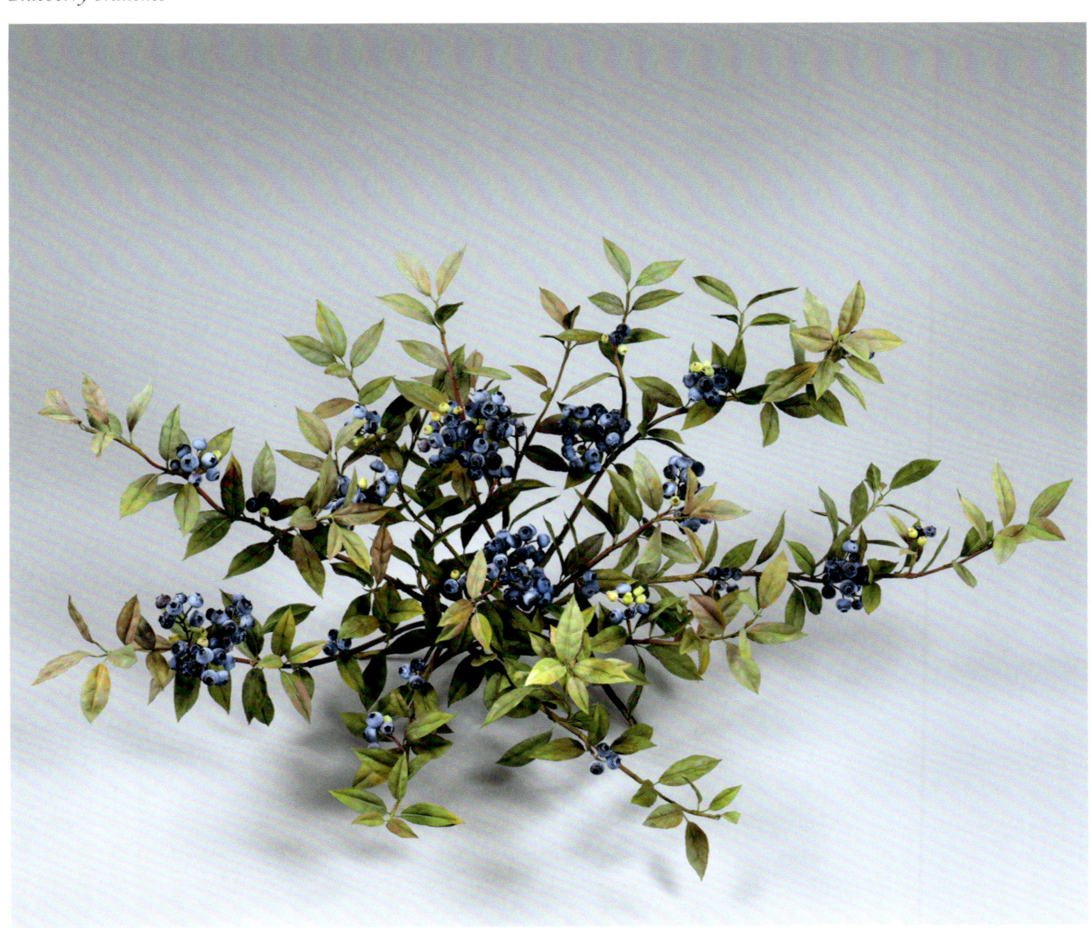

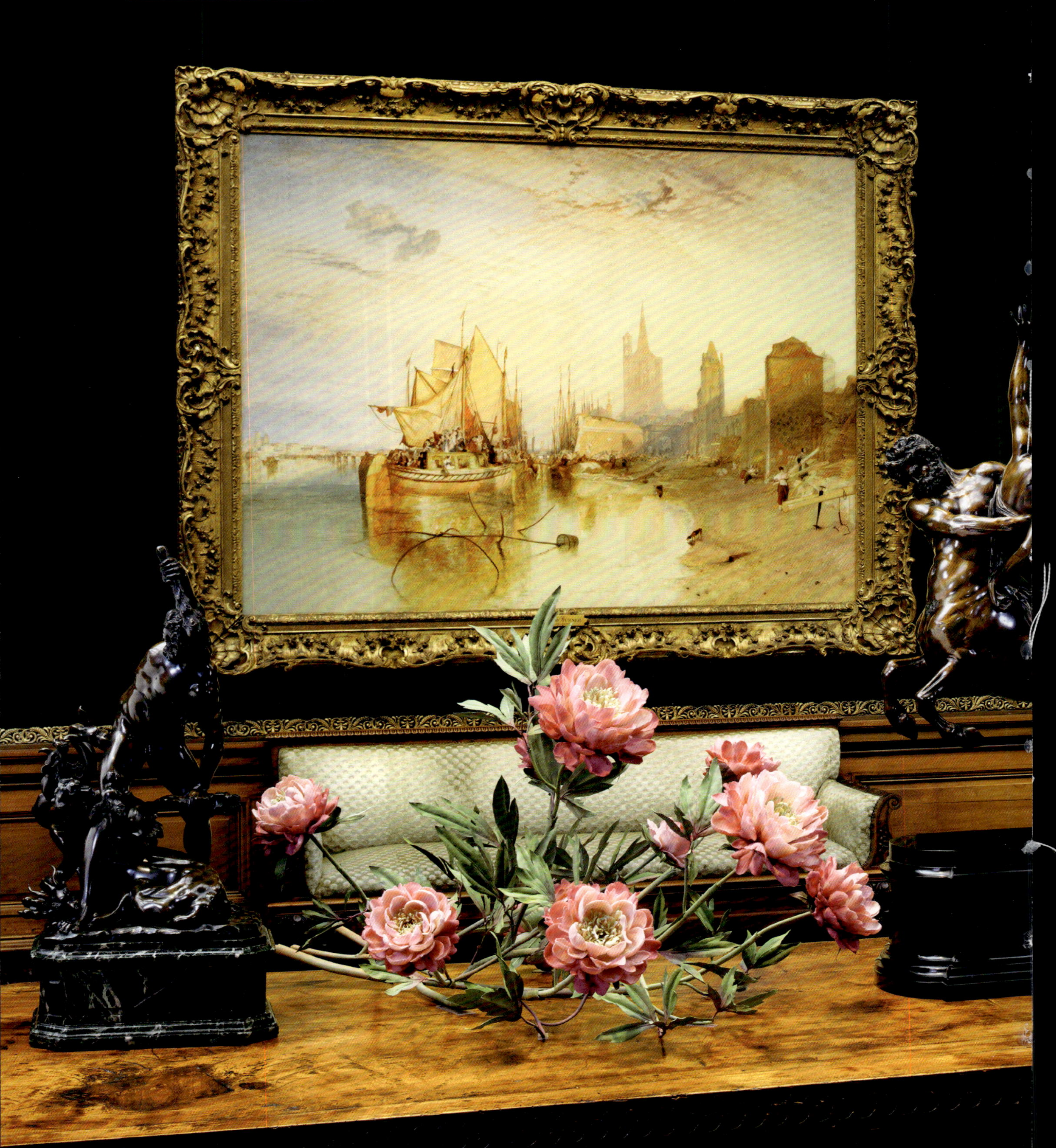

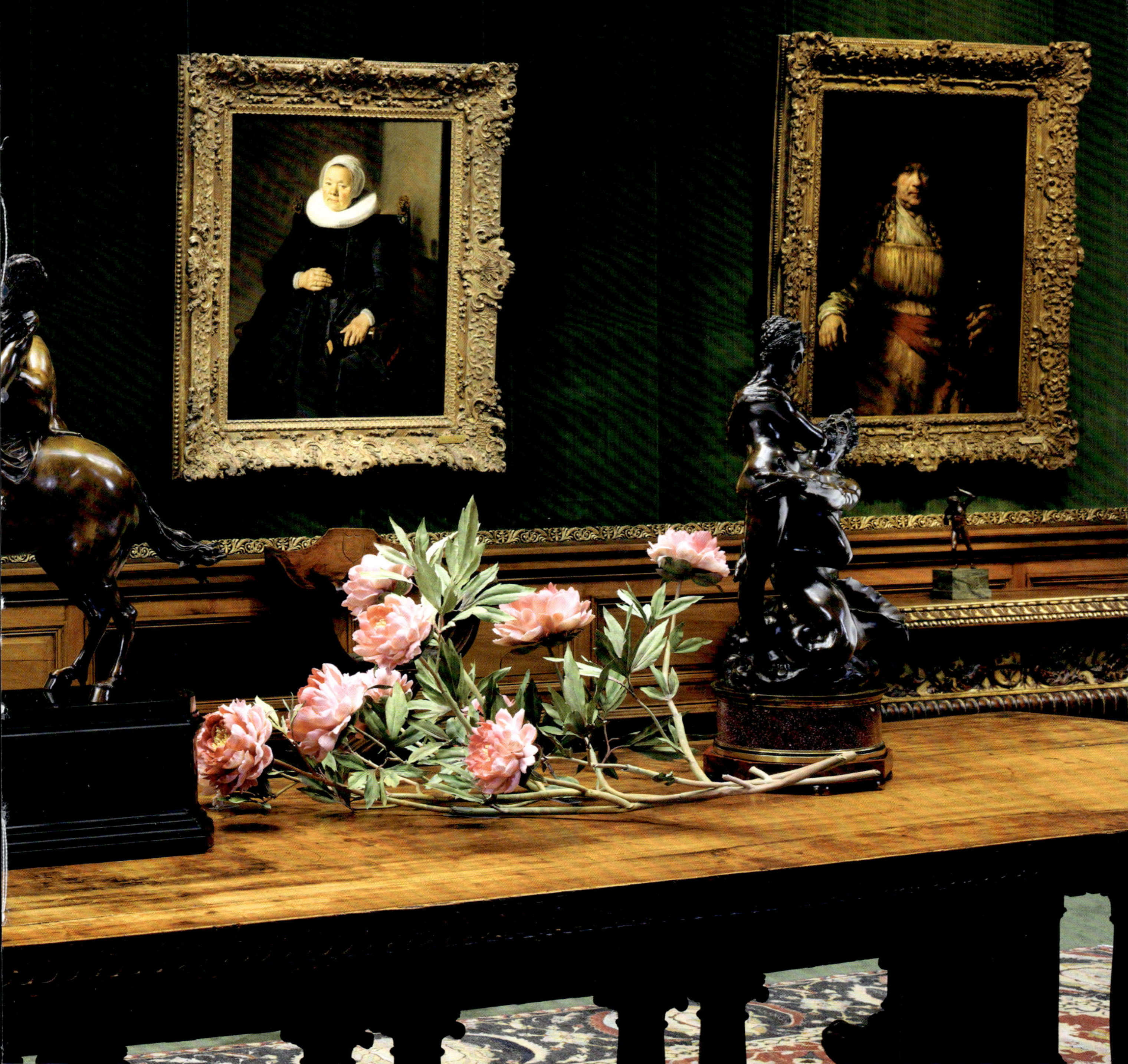

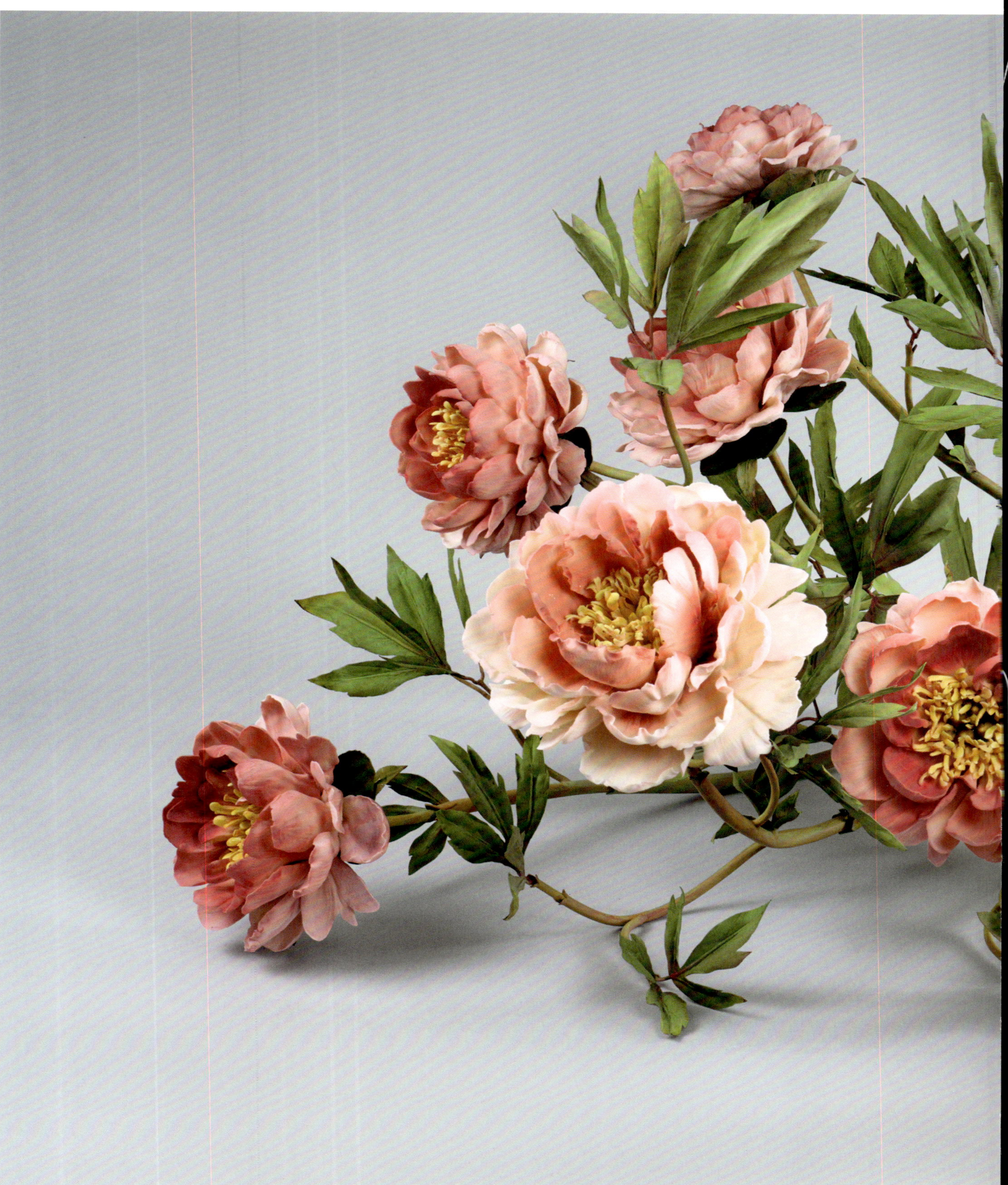

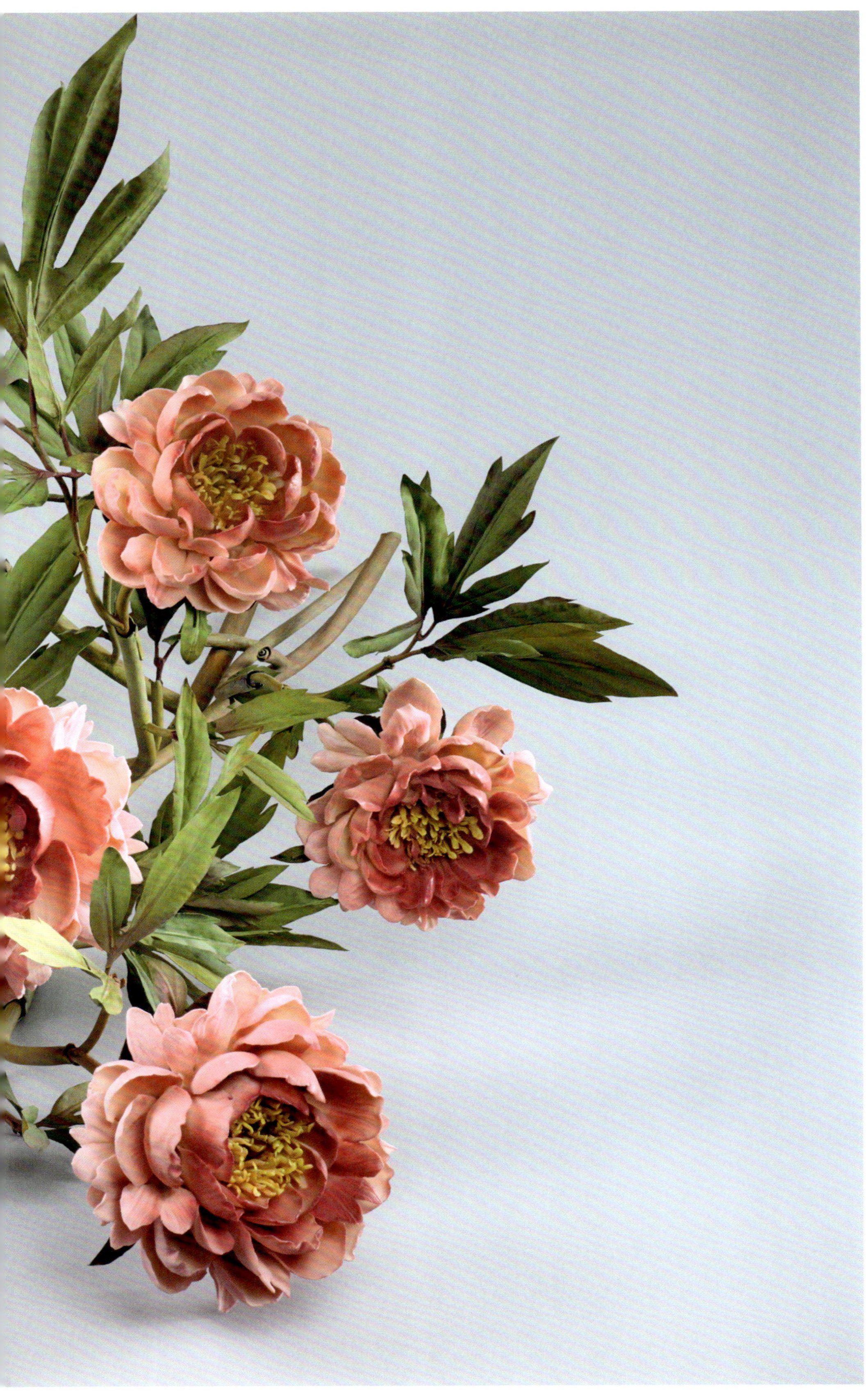

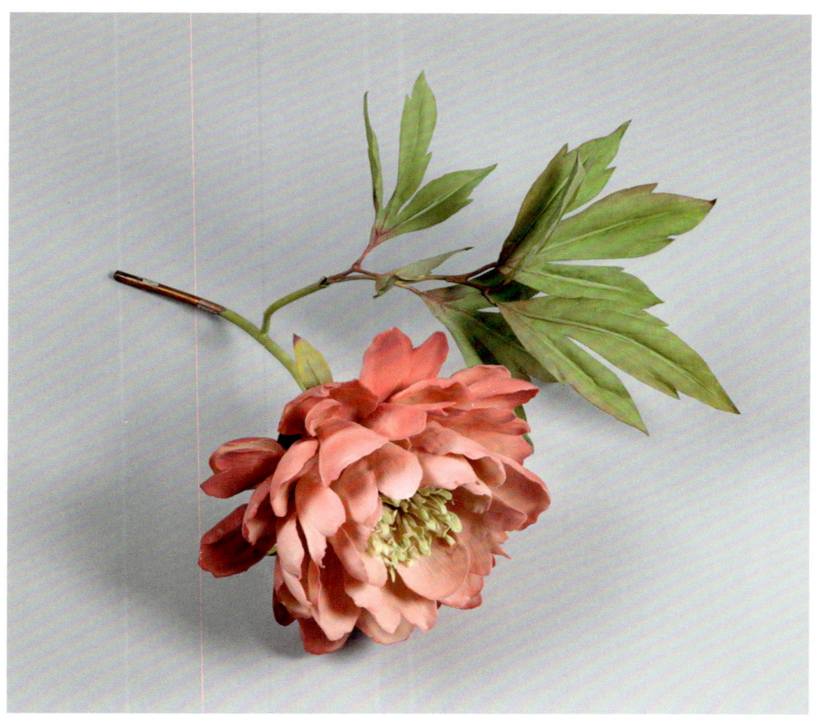

Peony bouquets

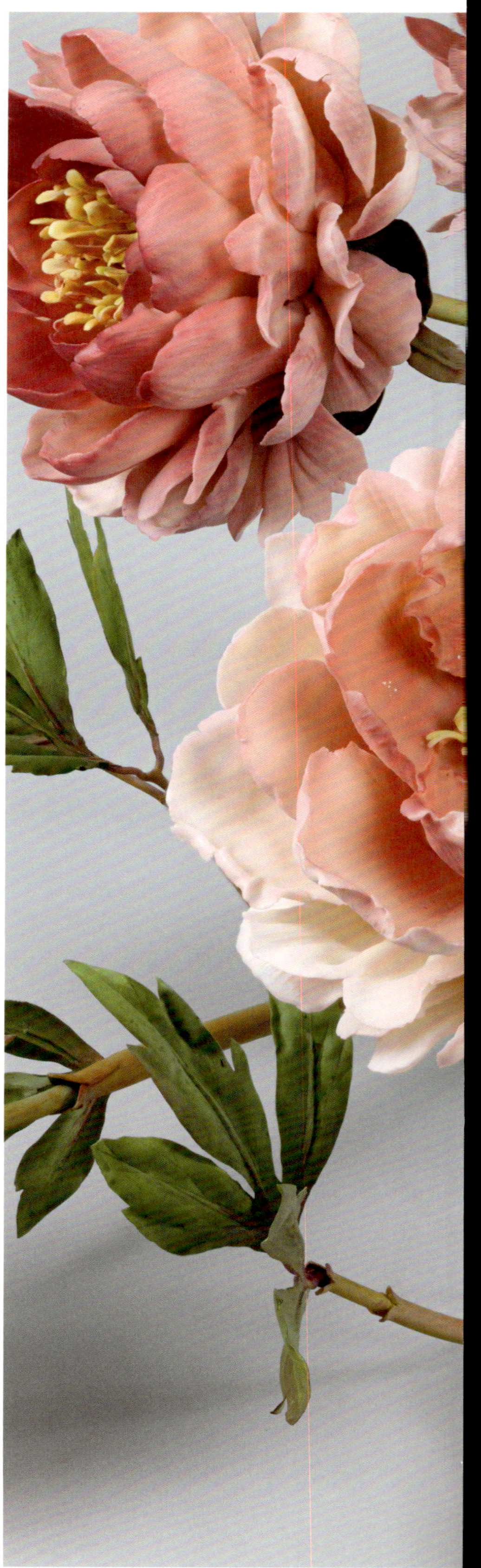

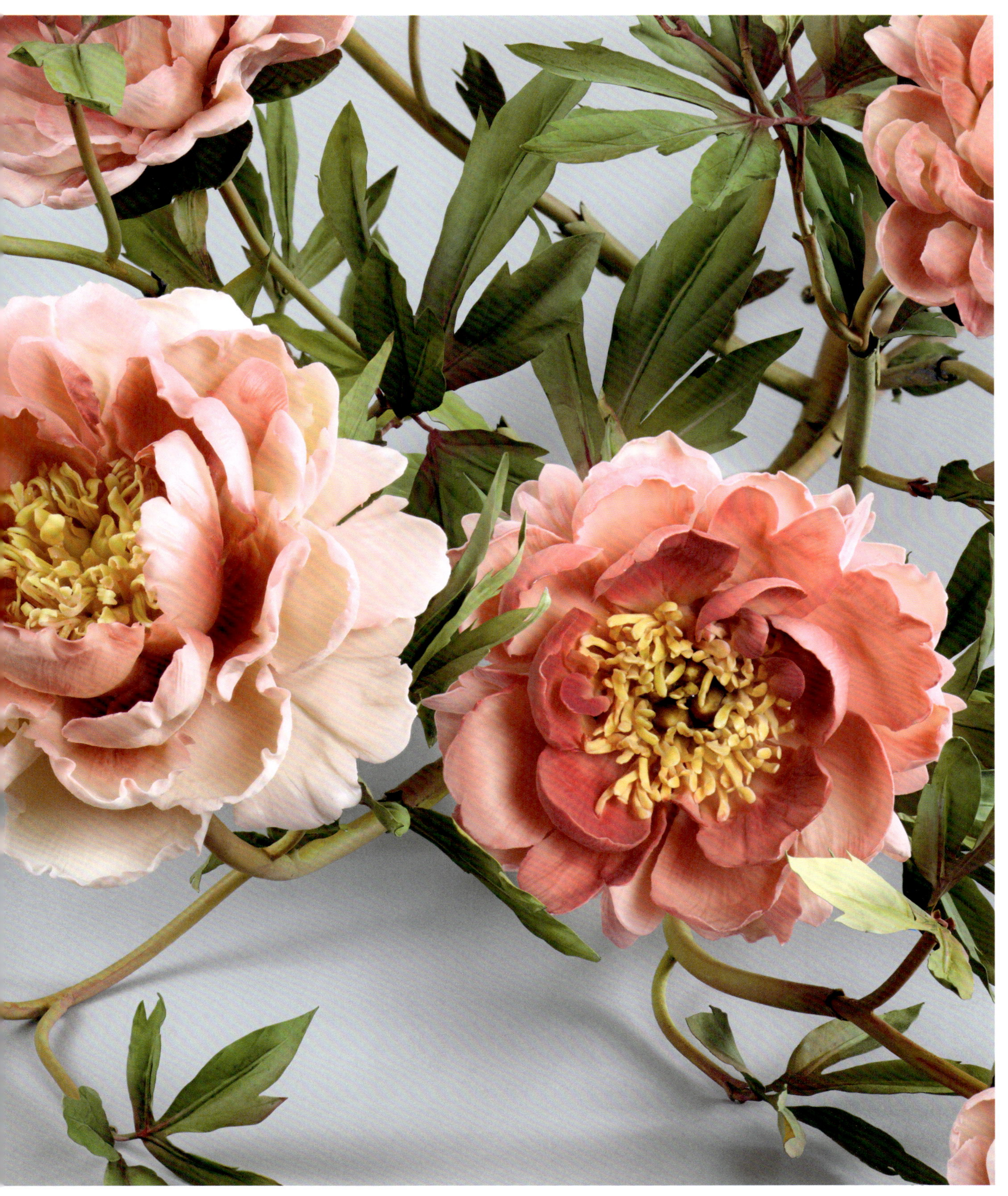

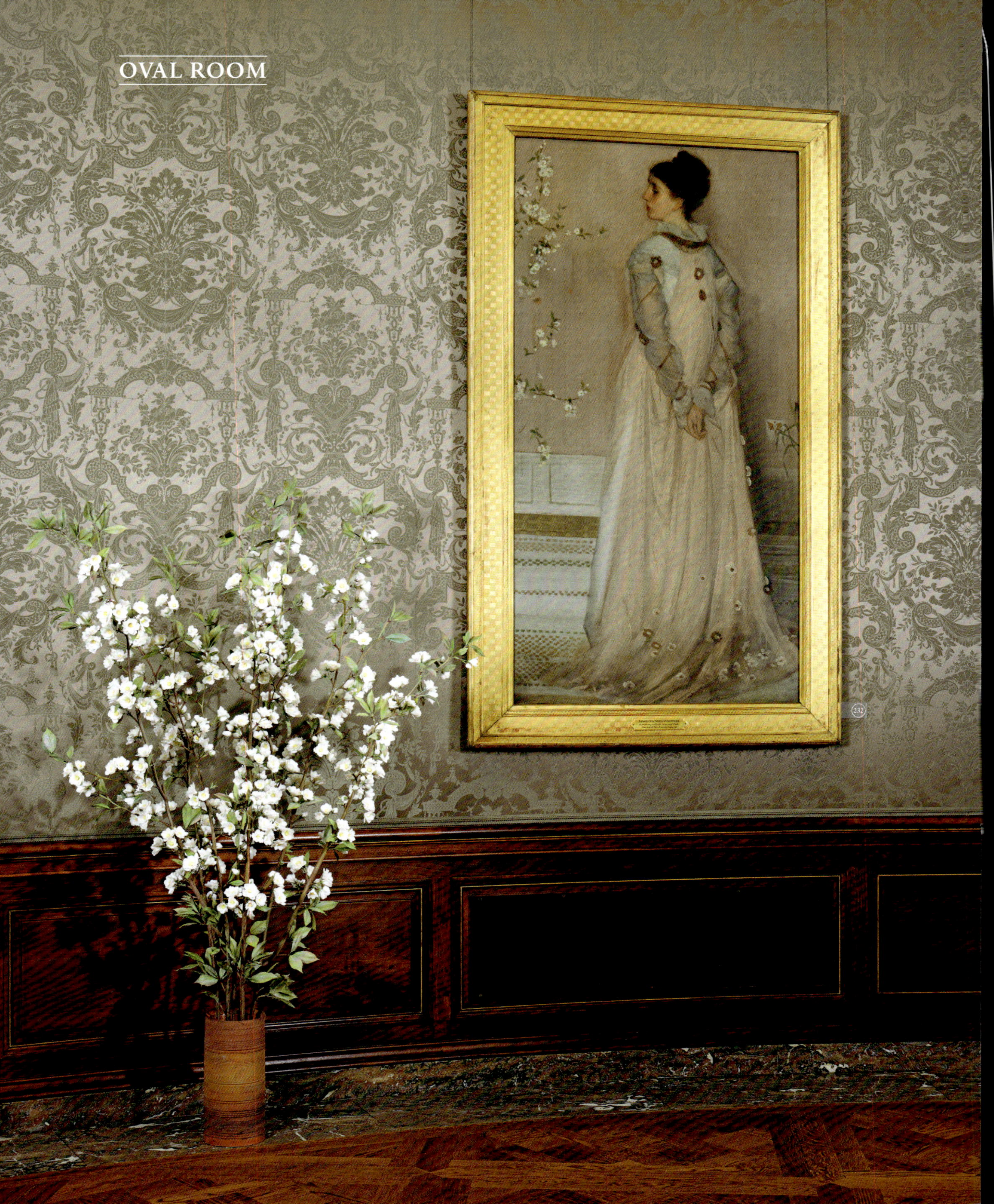

Cherry blossoms

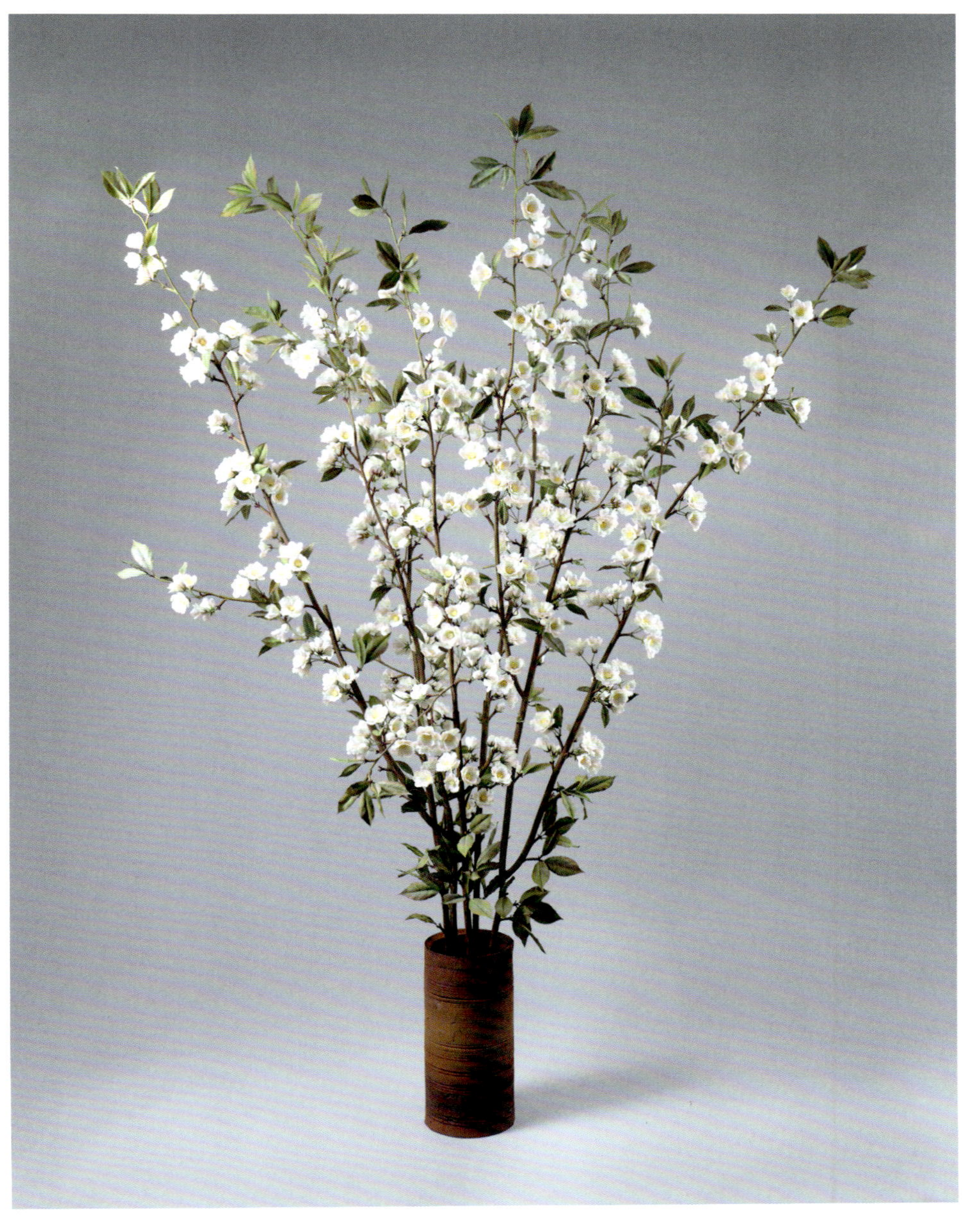

Cherry blossoms

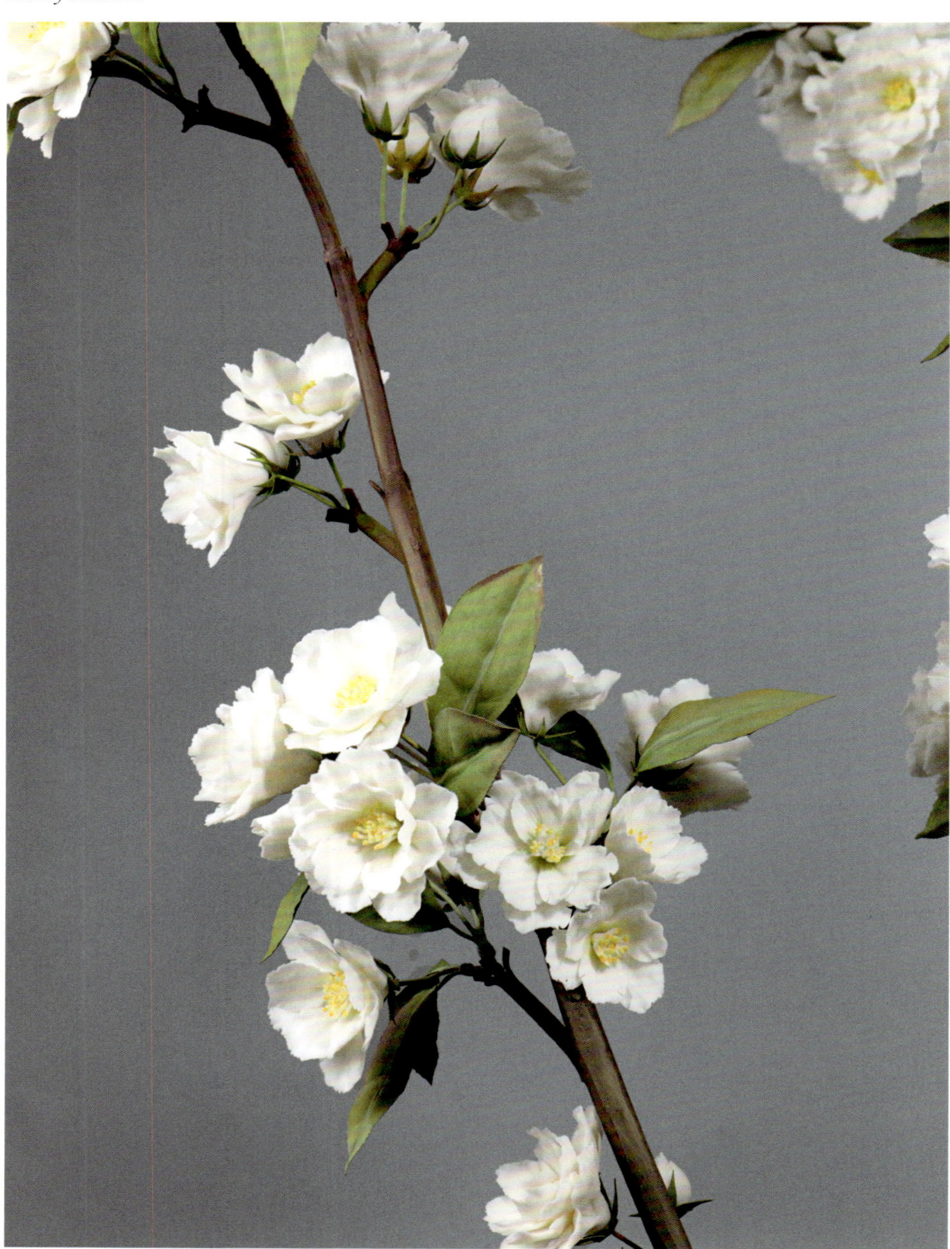

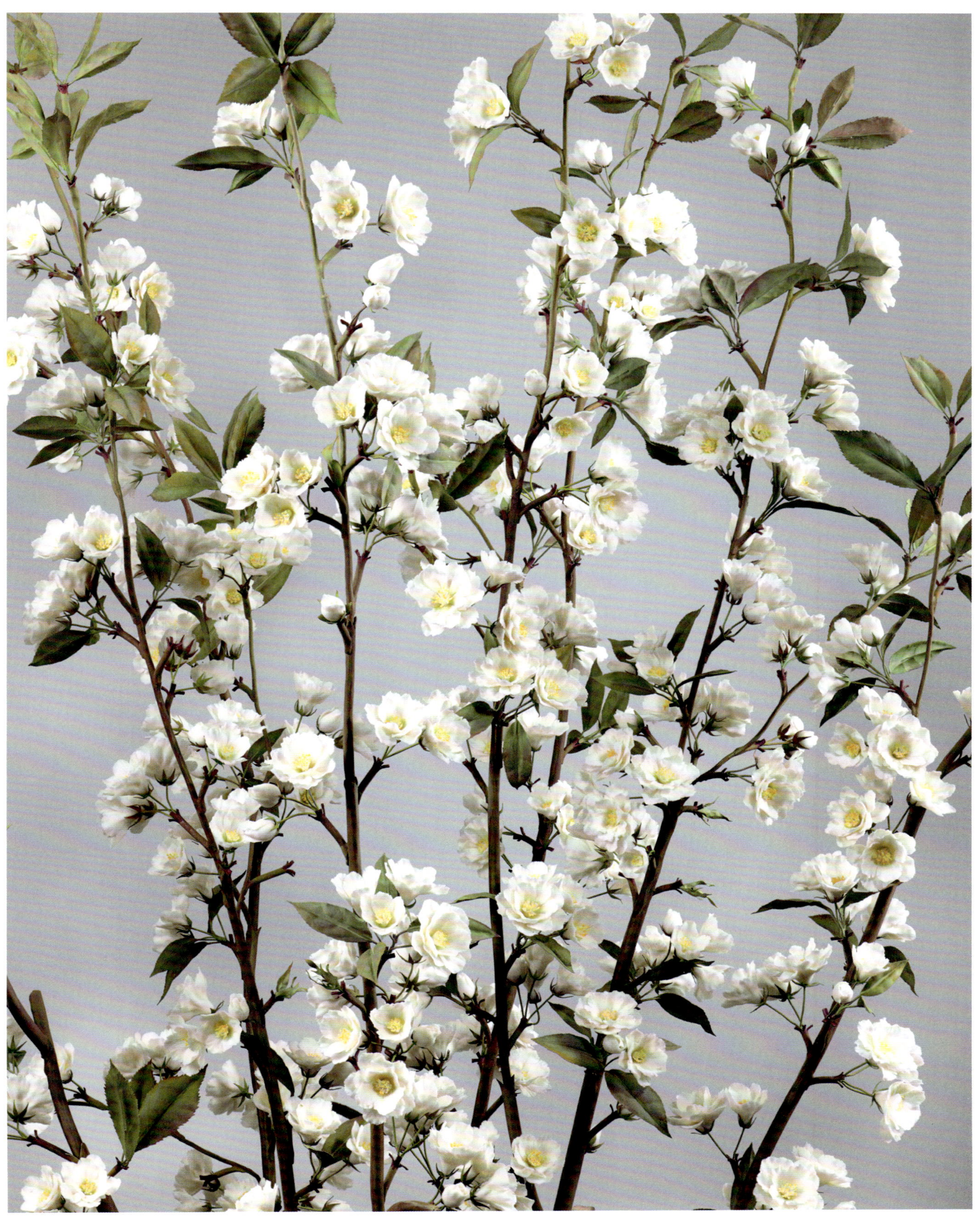

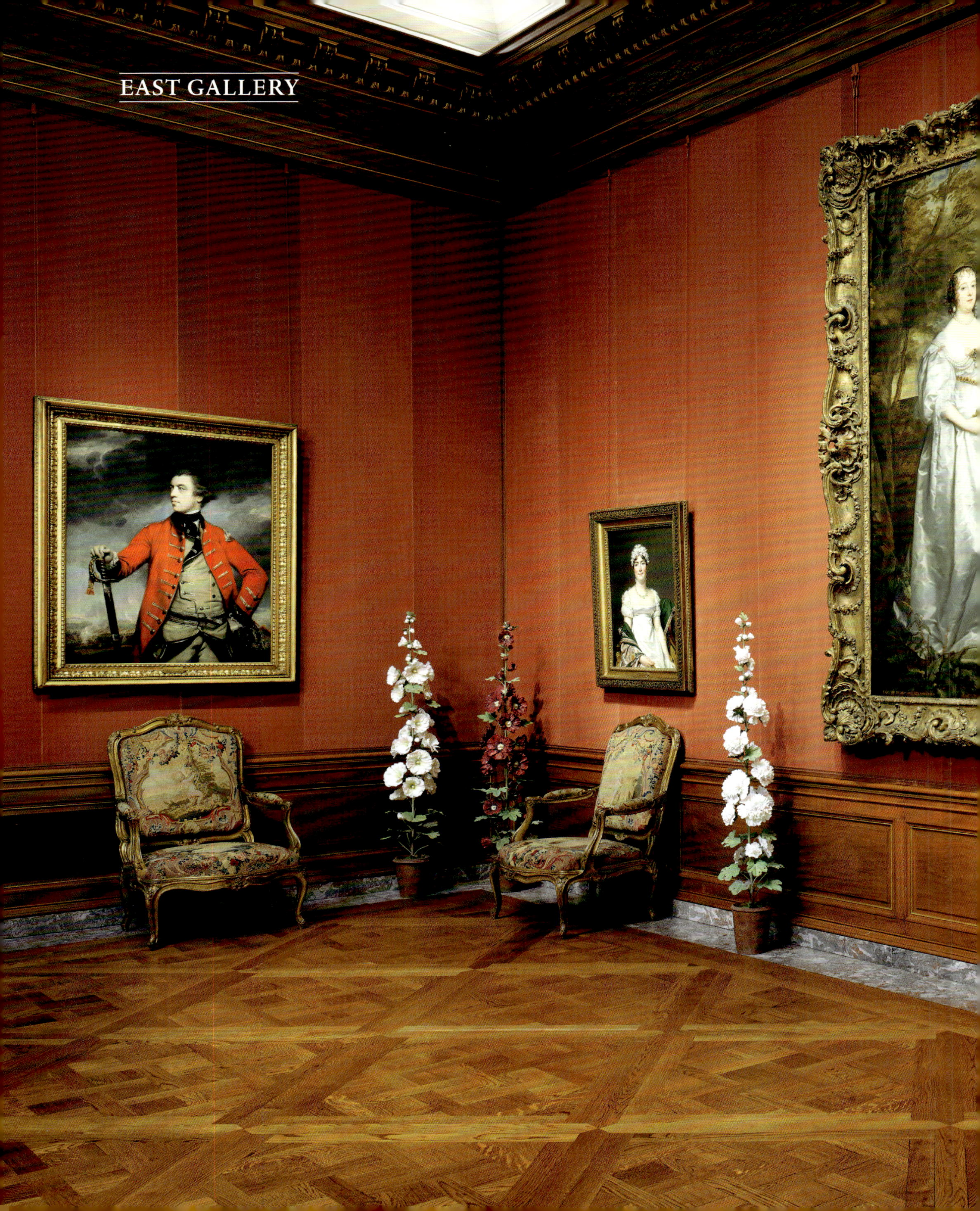
EAST GALLERY

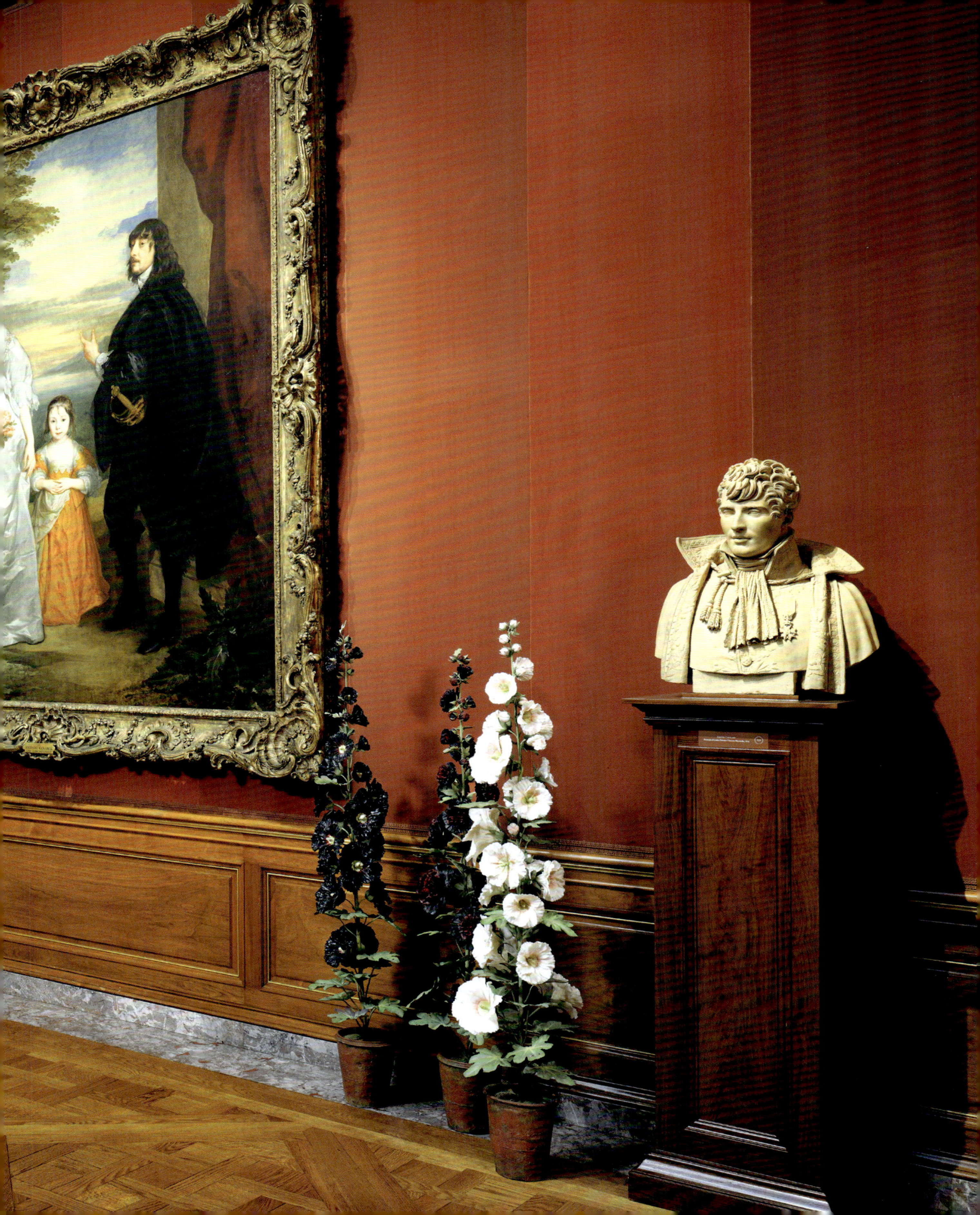

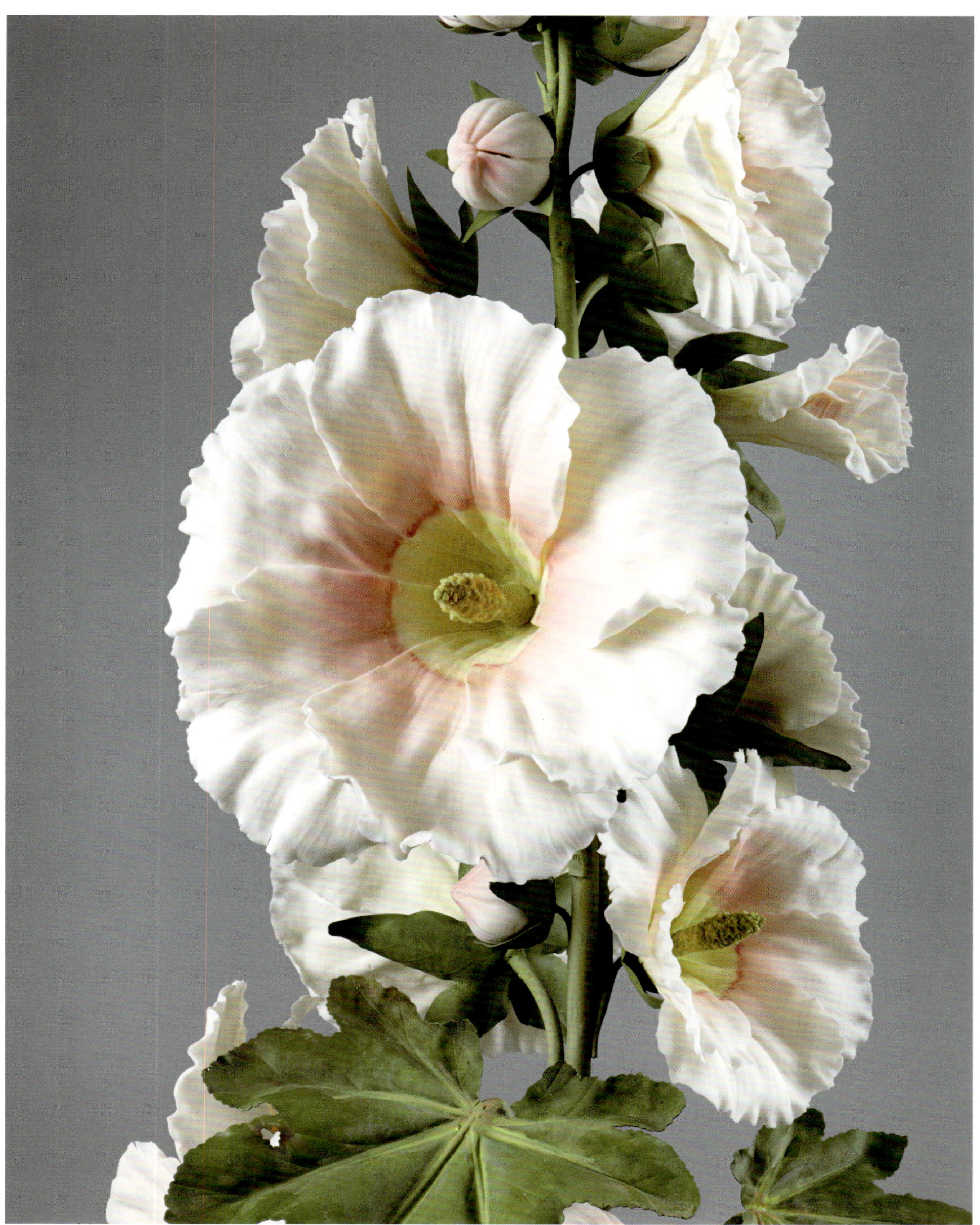

Hollyhocks

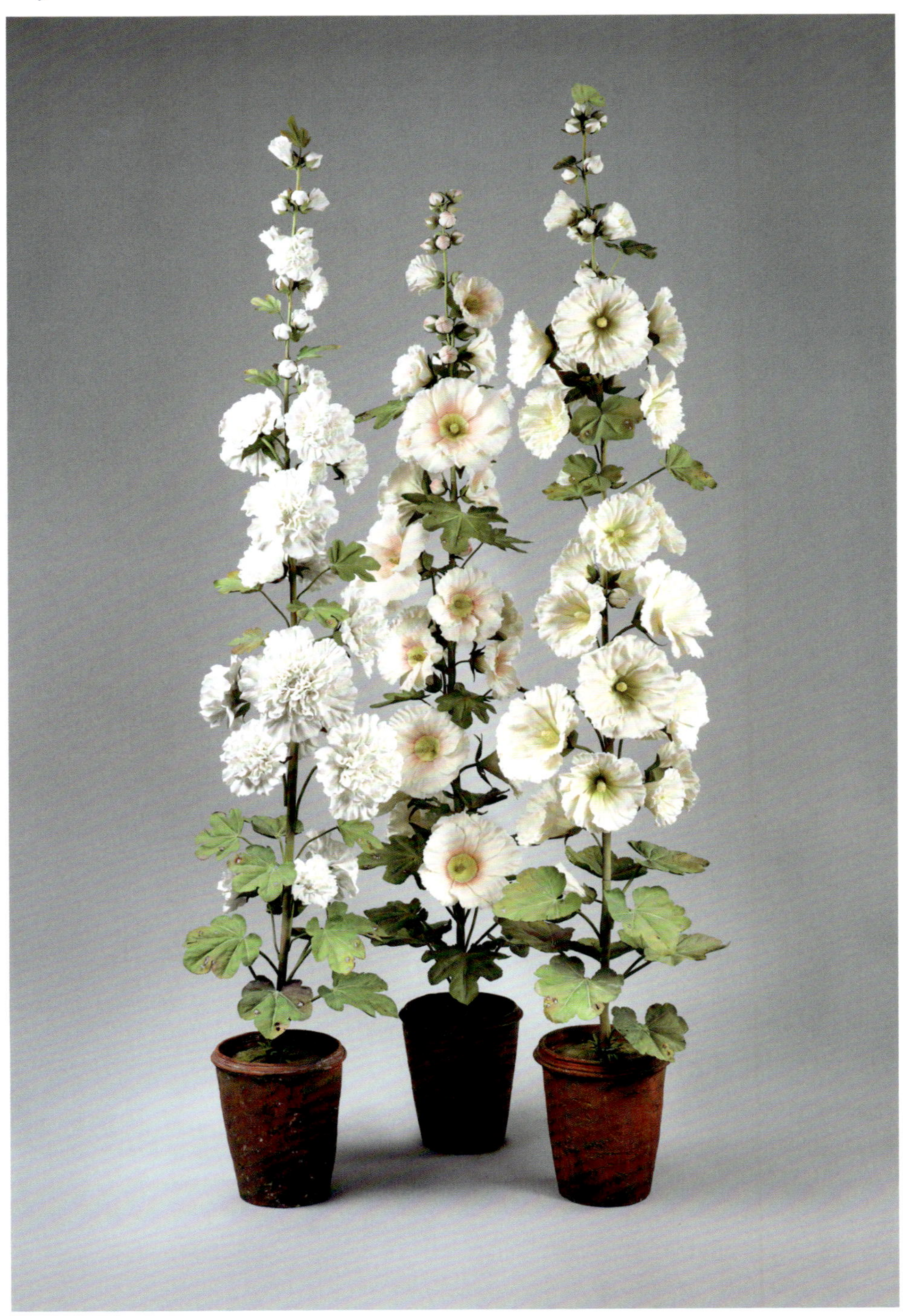

Hollyhocks

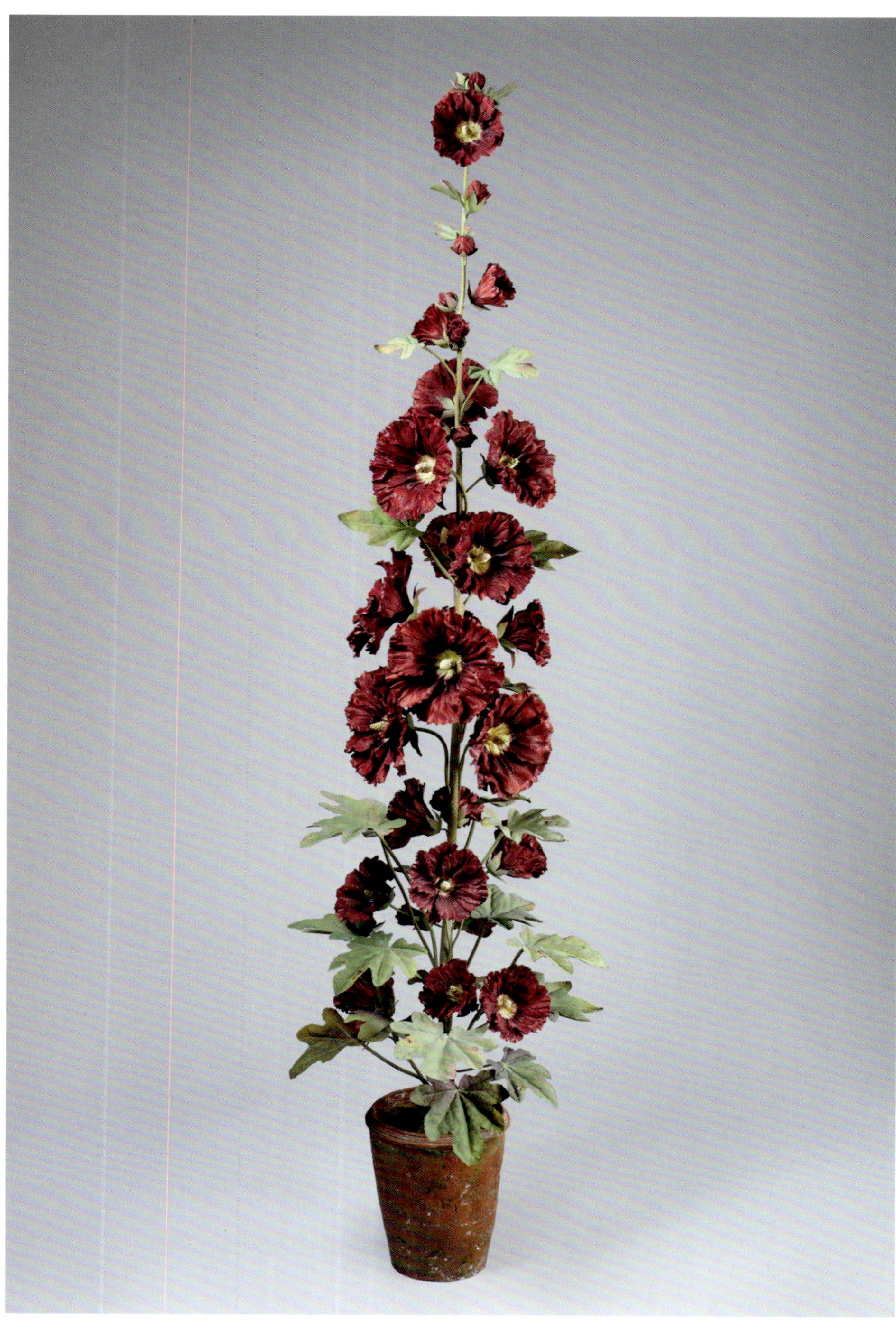

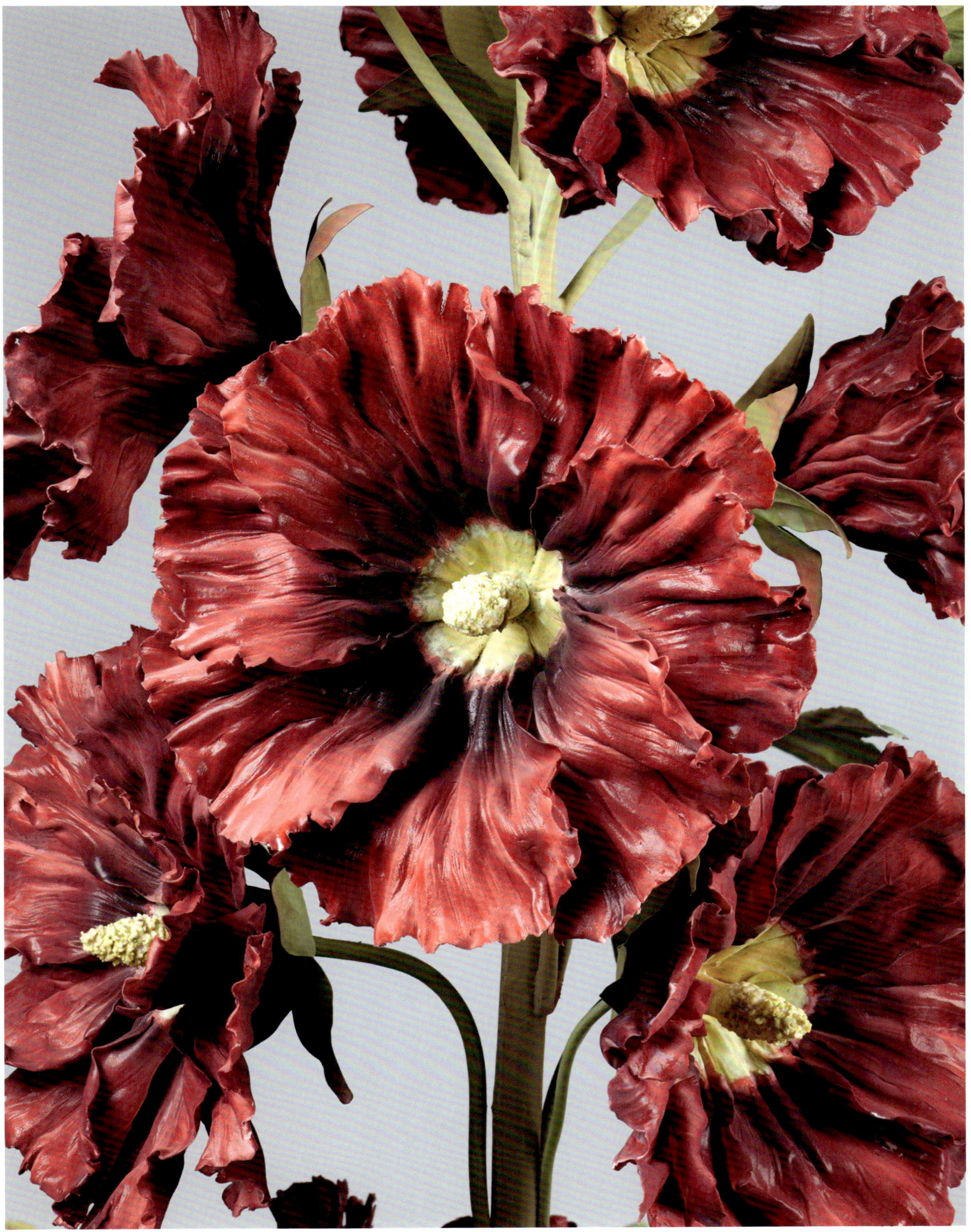

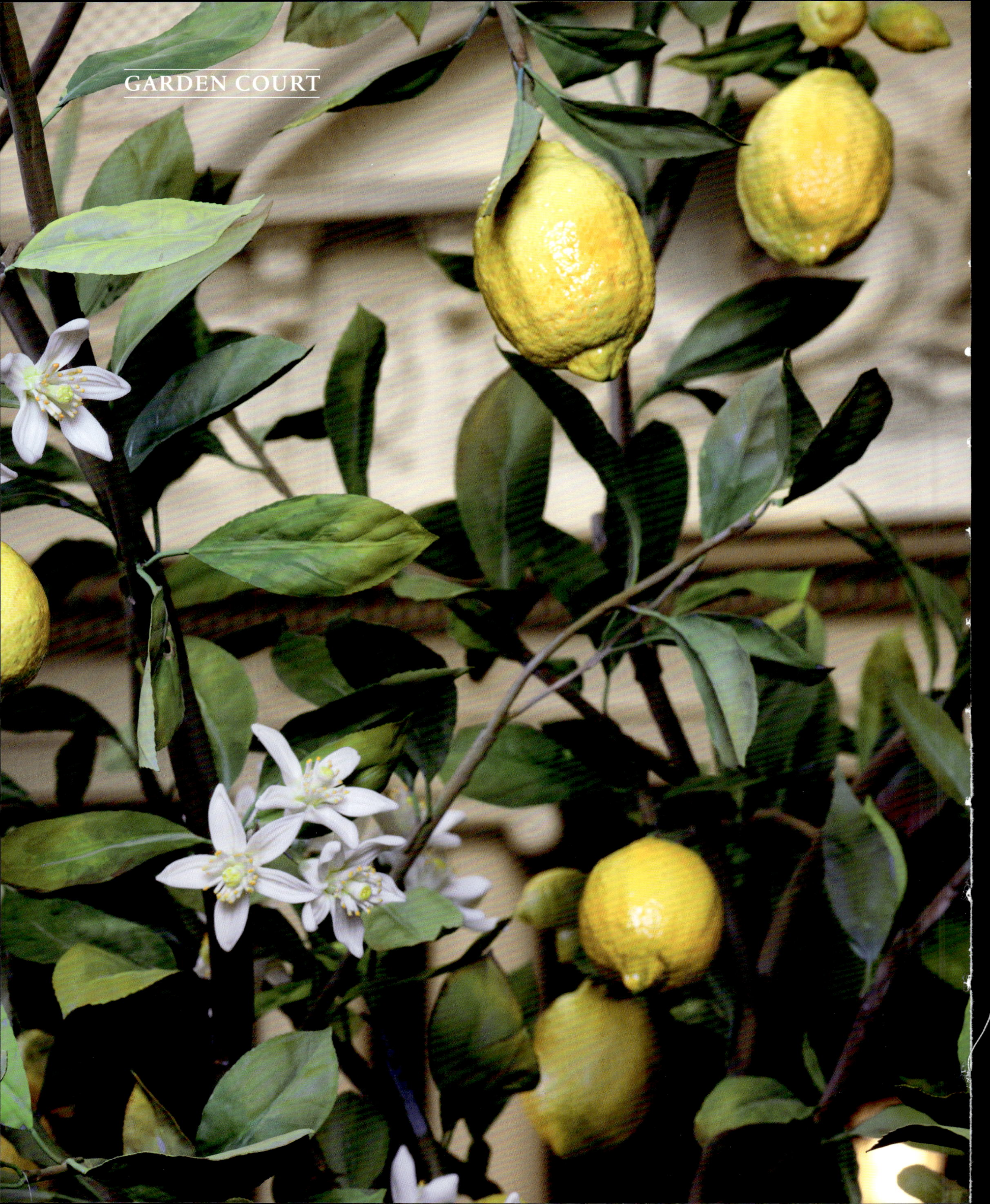
GARDEN COURT

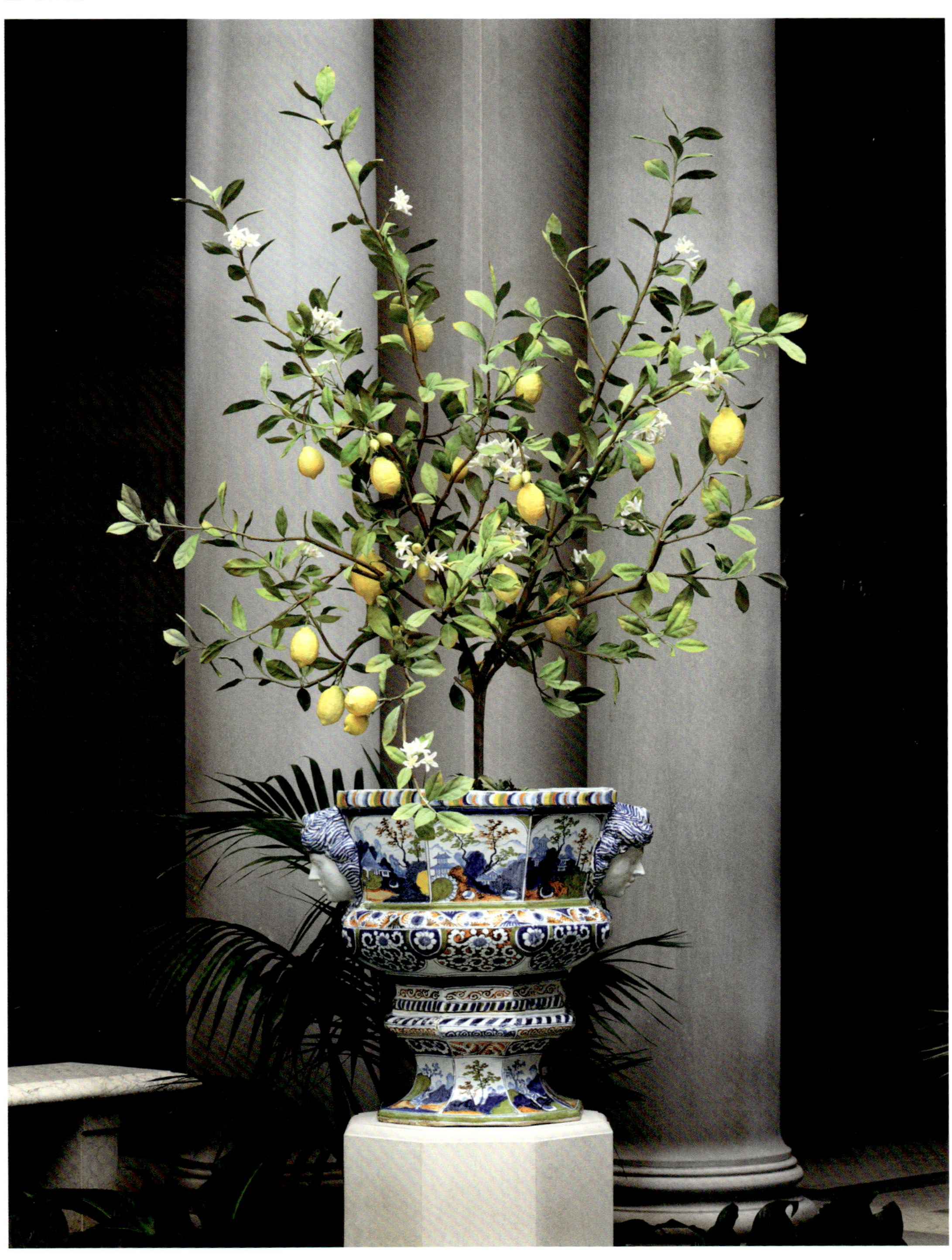

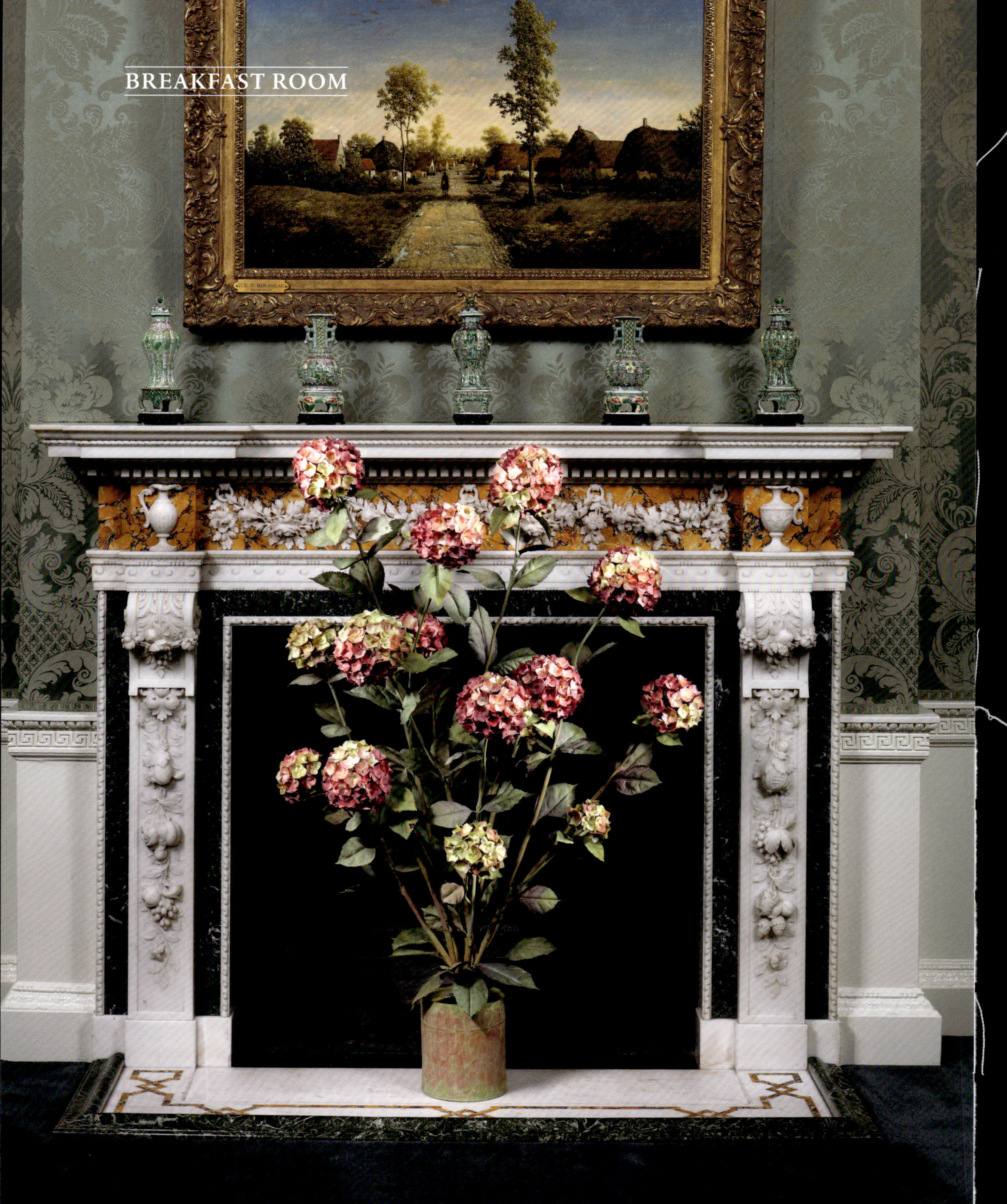

Hydrangeas

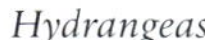

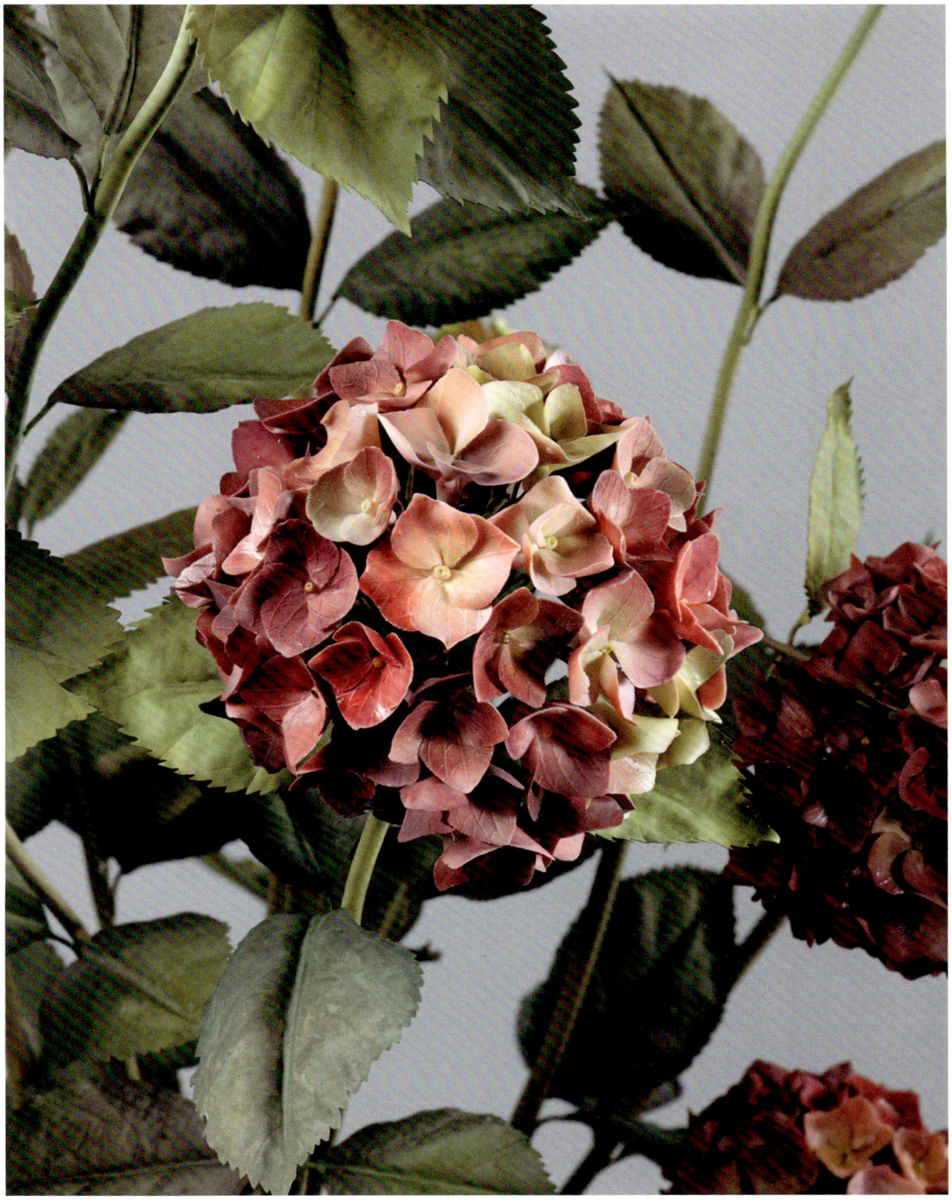

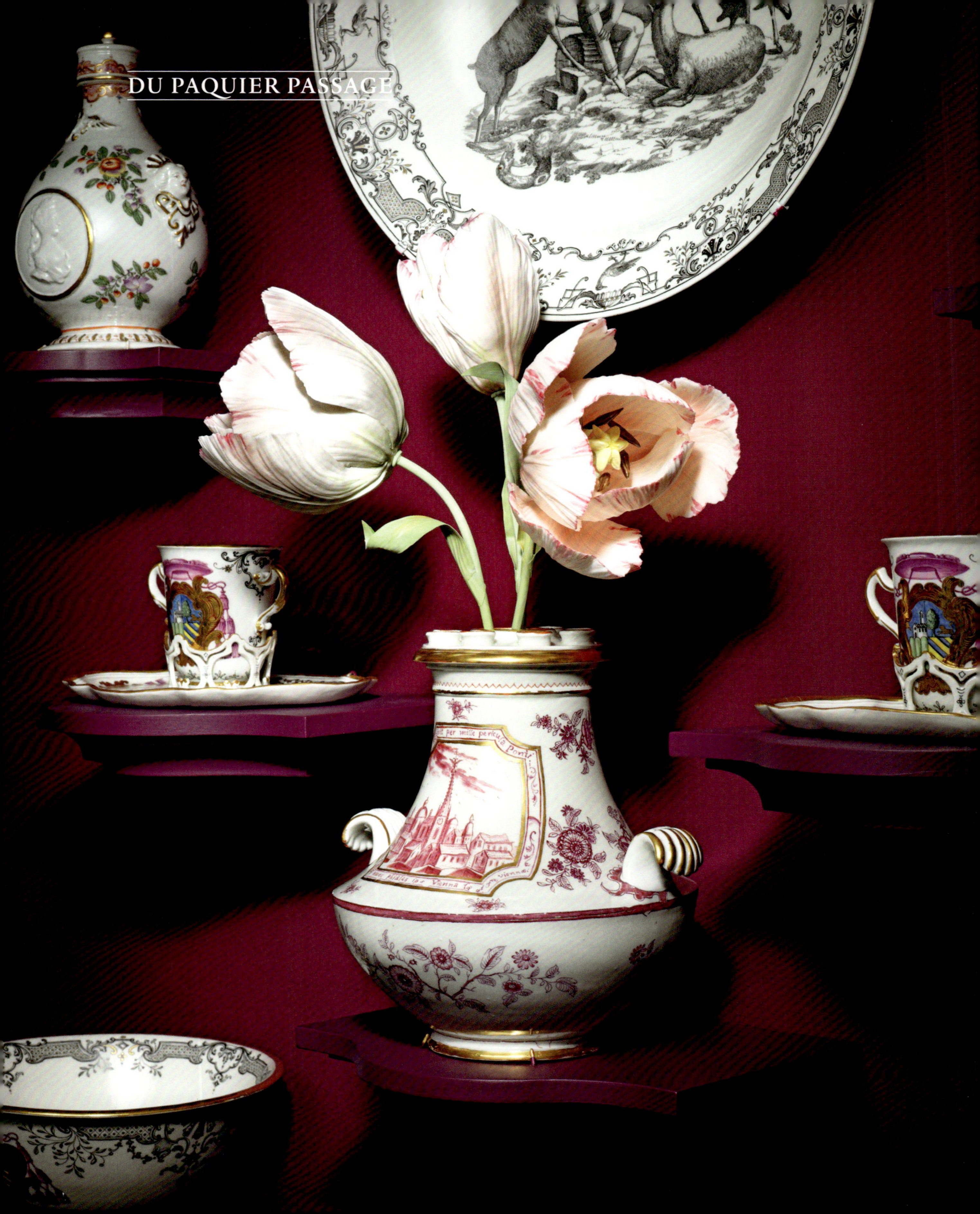
DU PAQUIER PASSAGE

Tulip stems

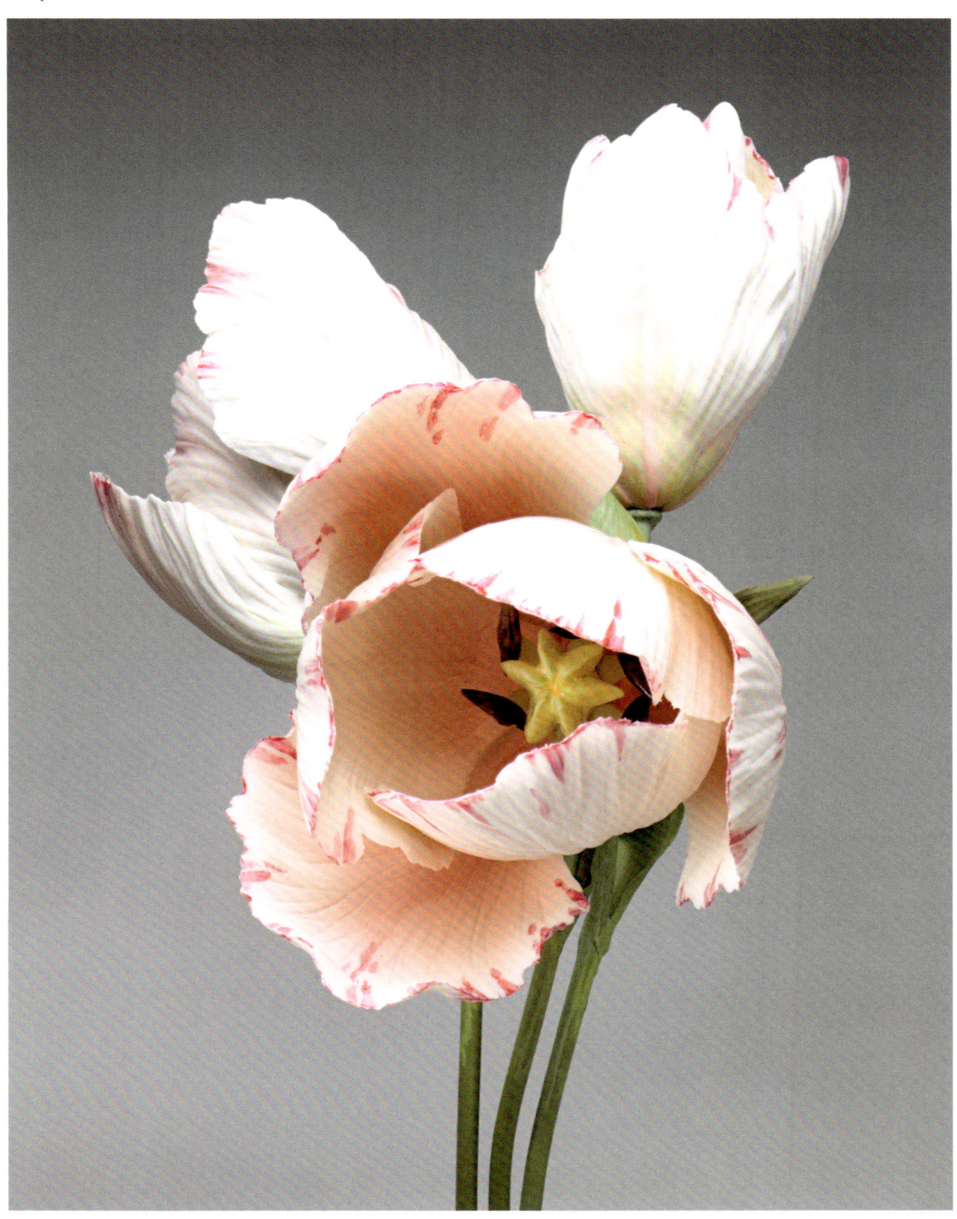

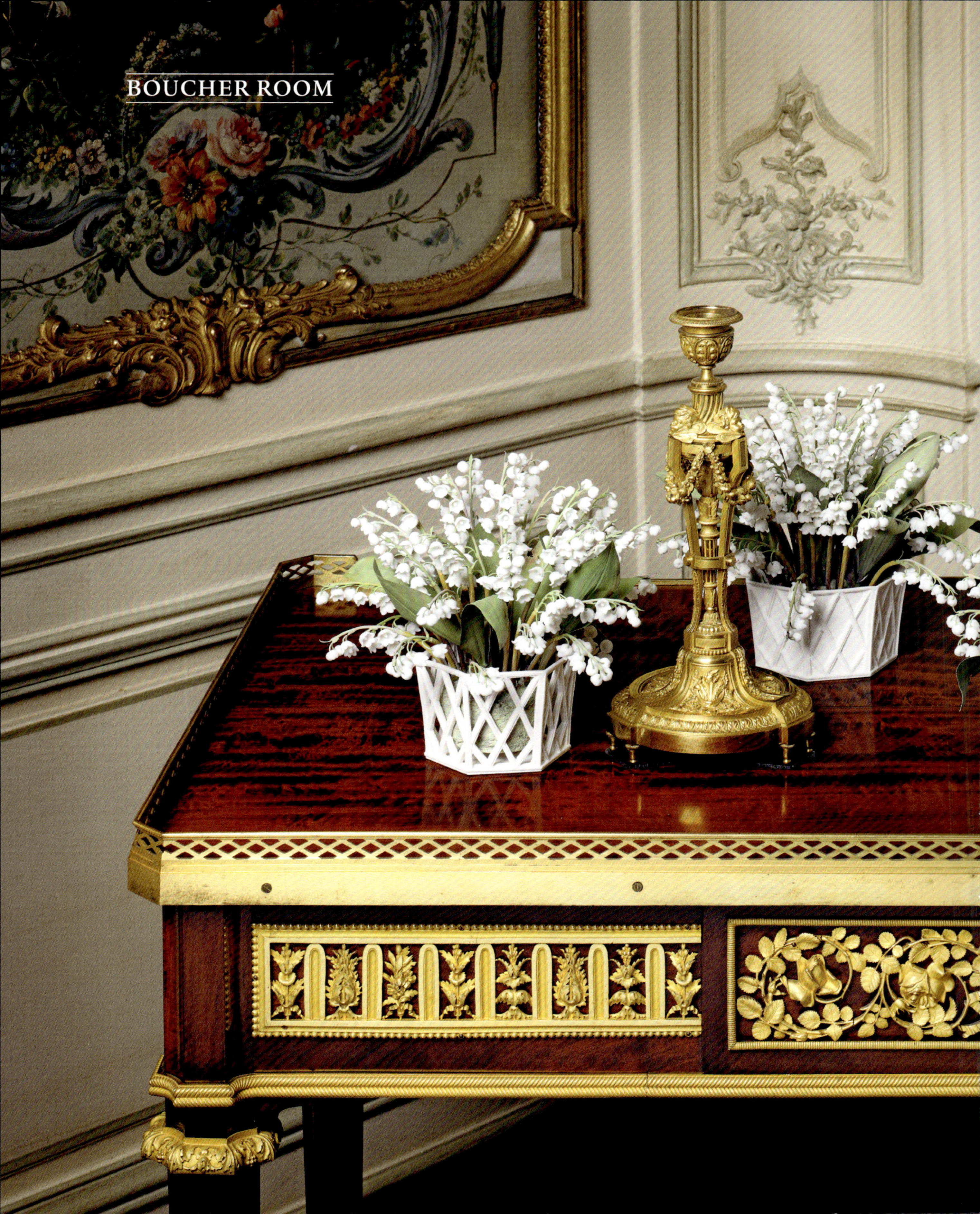

BOUCHER ROOM

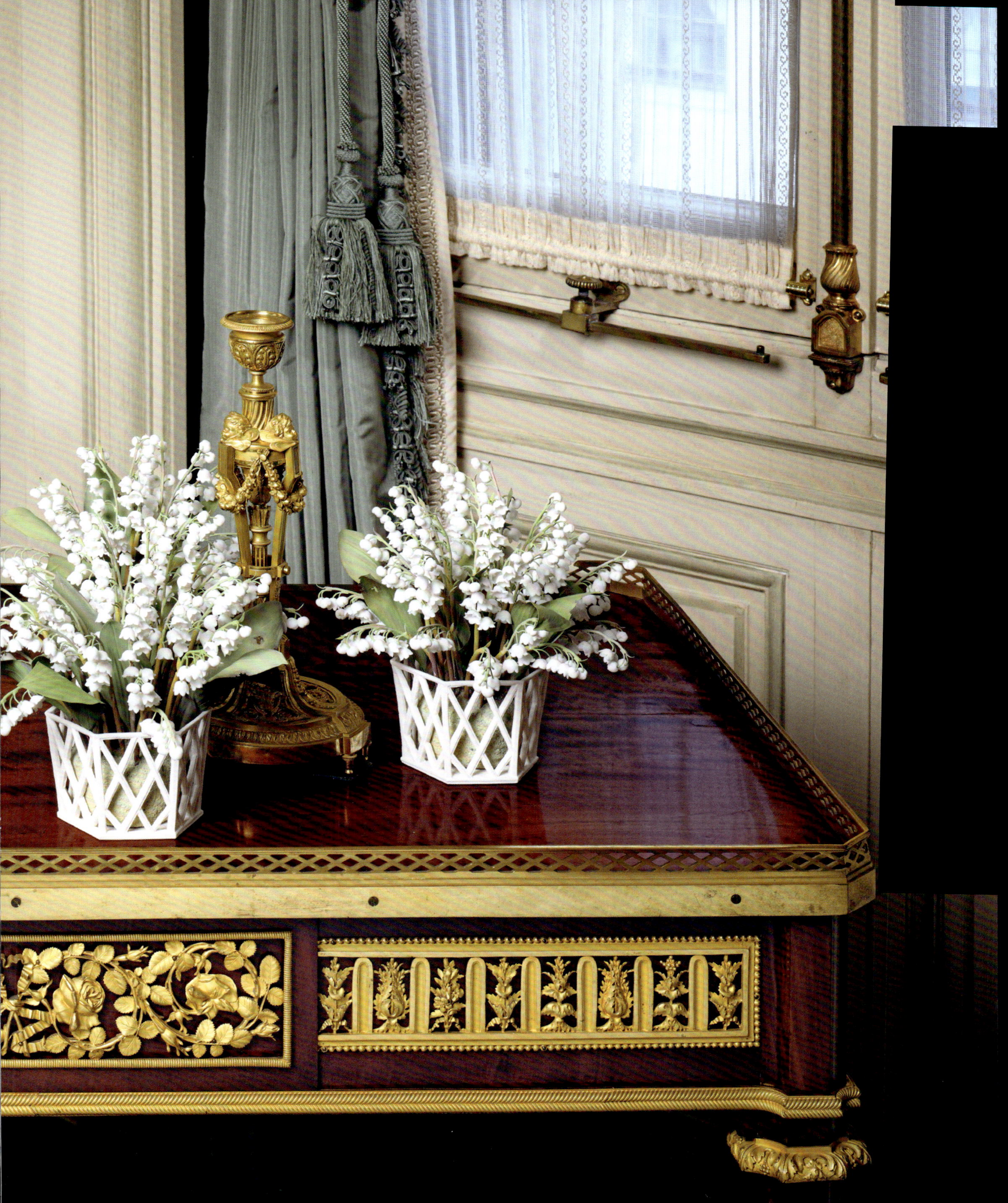

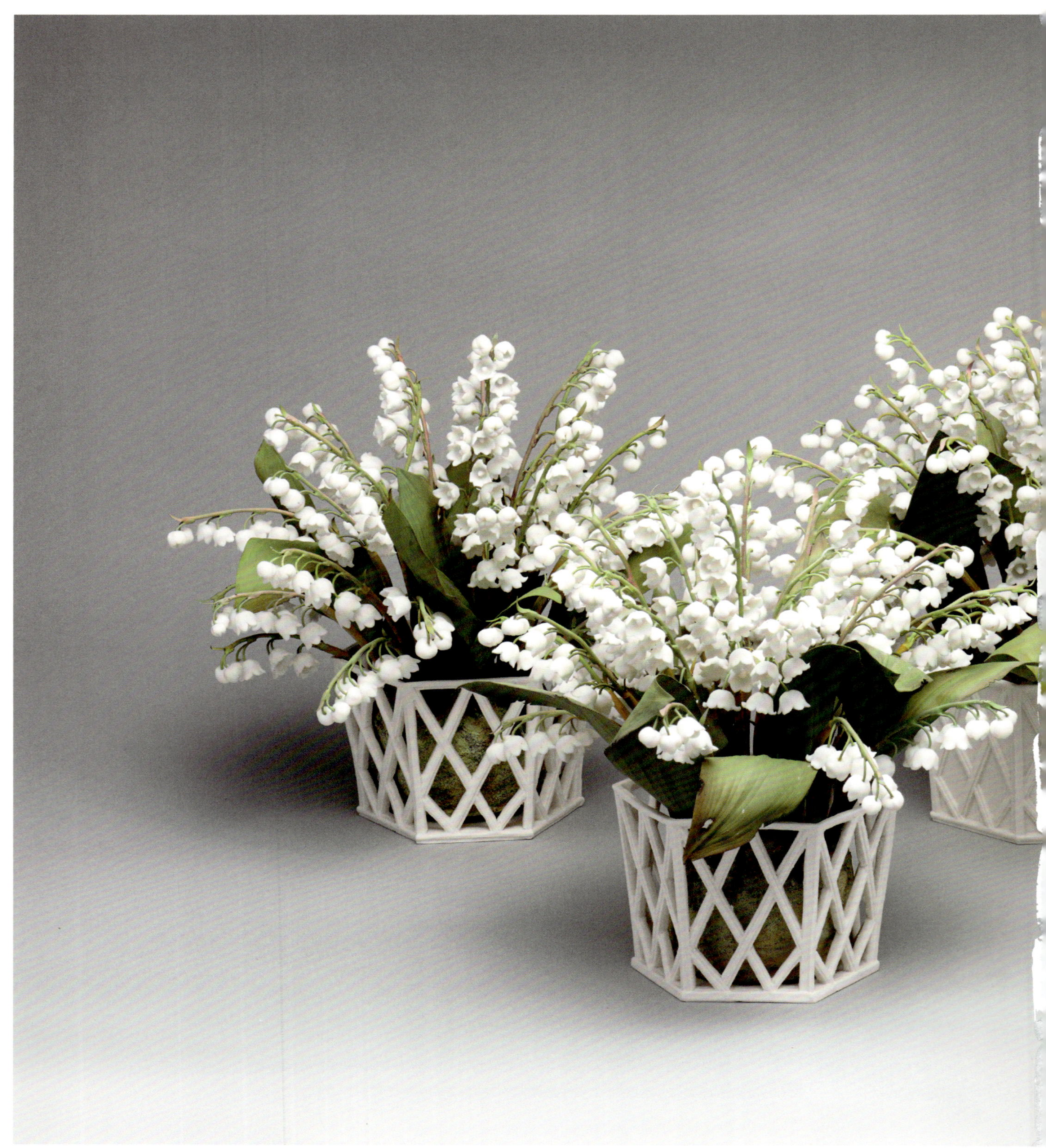

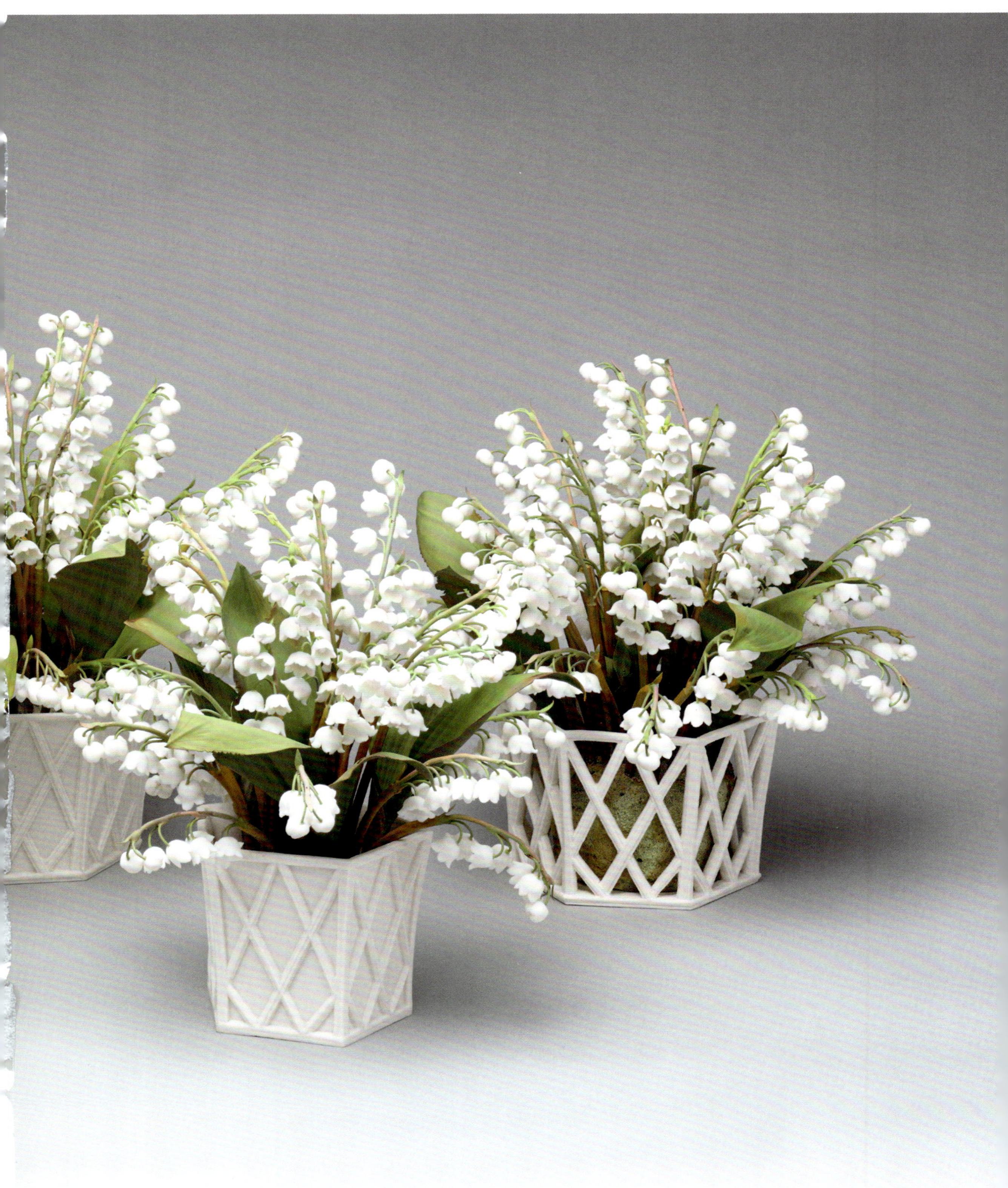

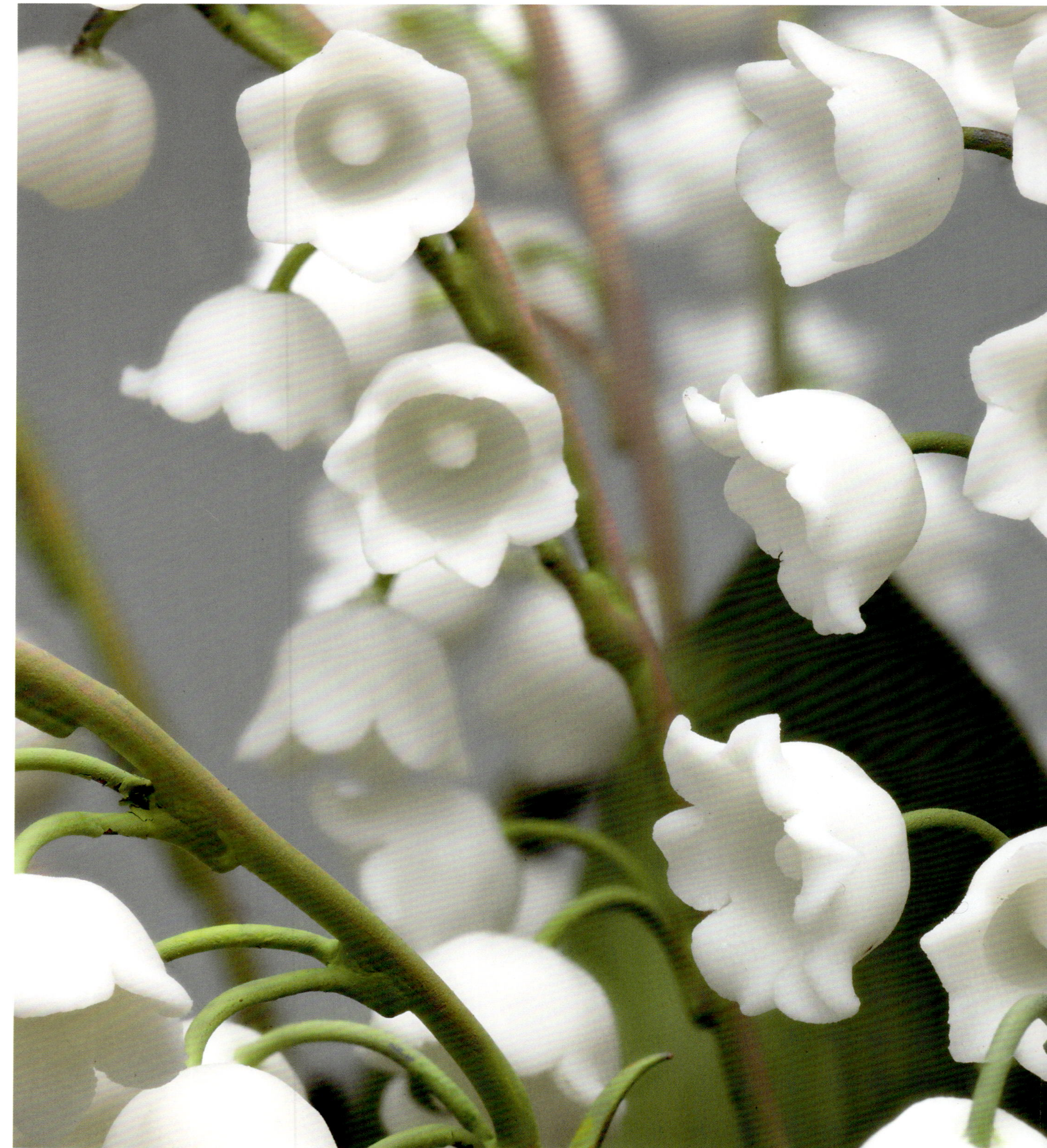

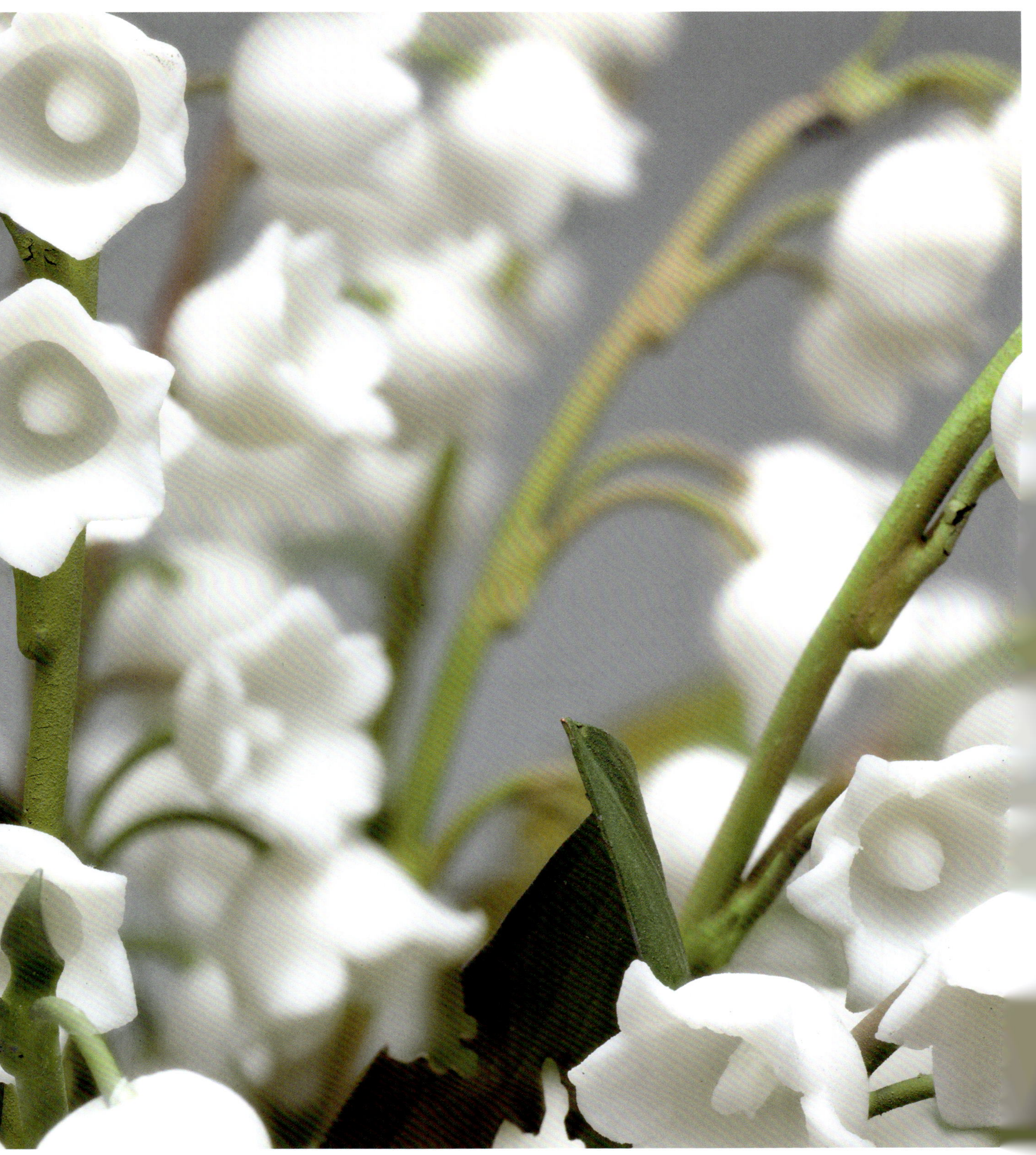

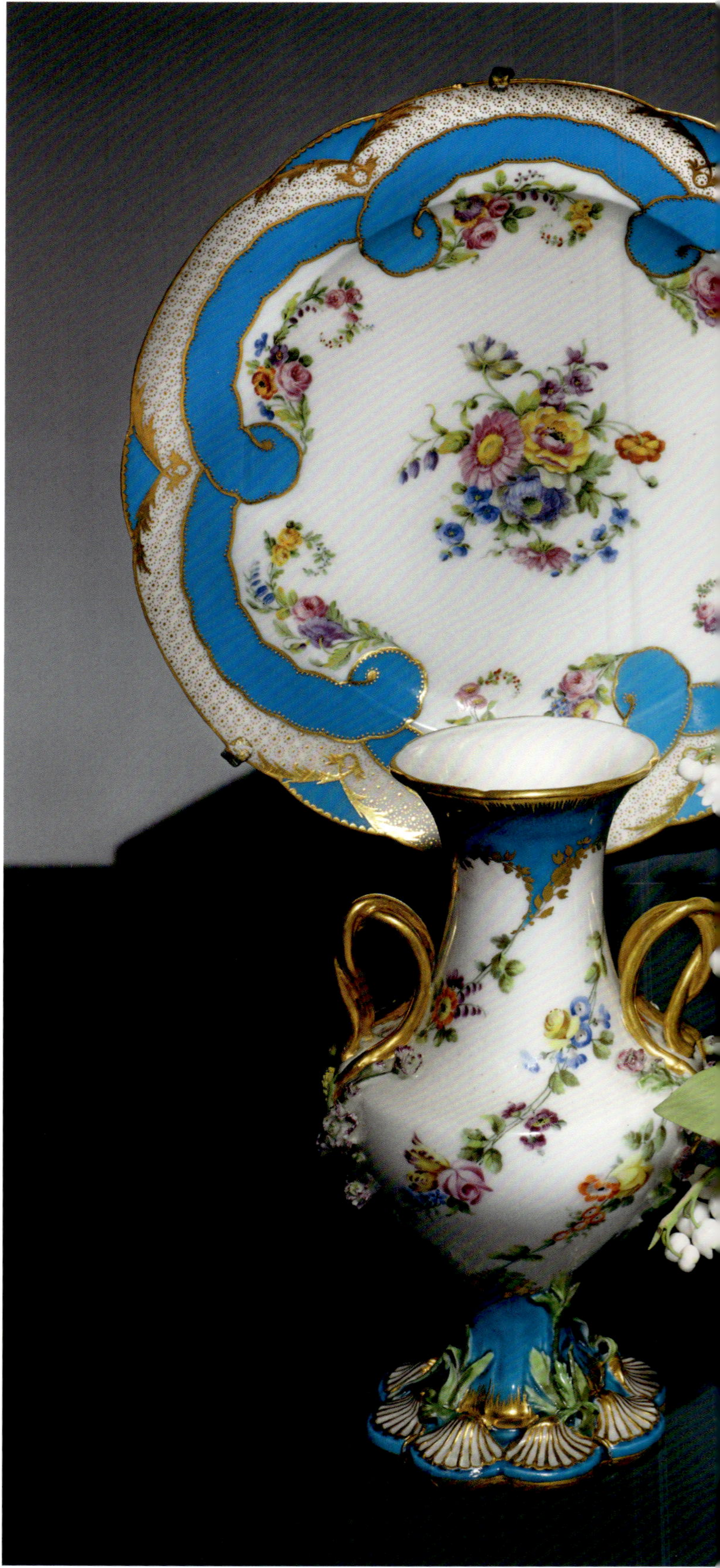

Lilies of the valley

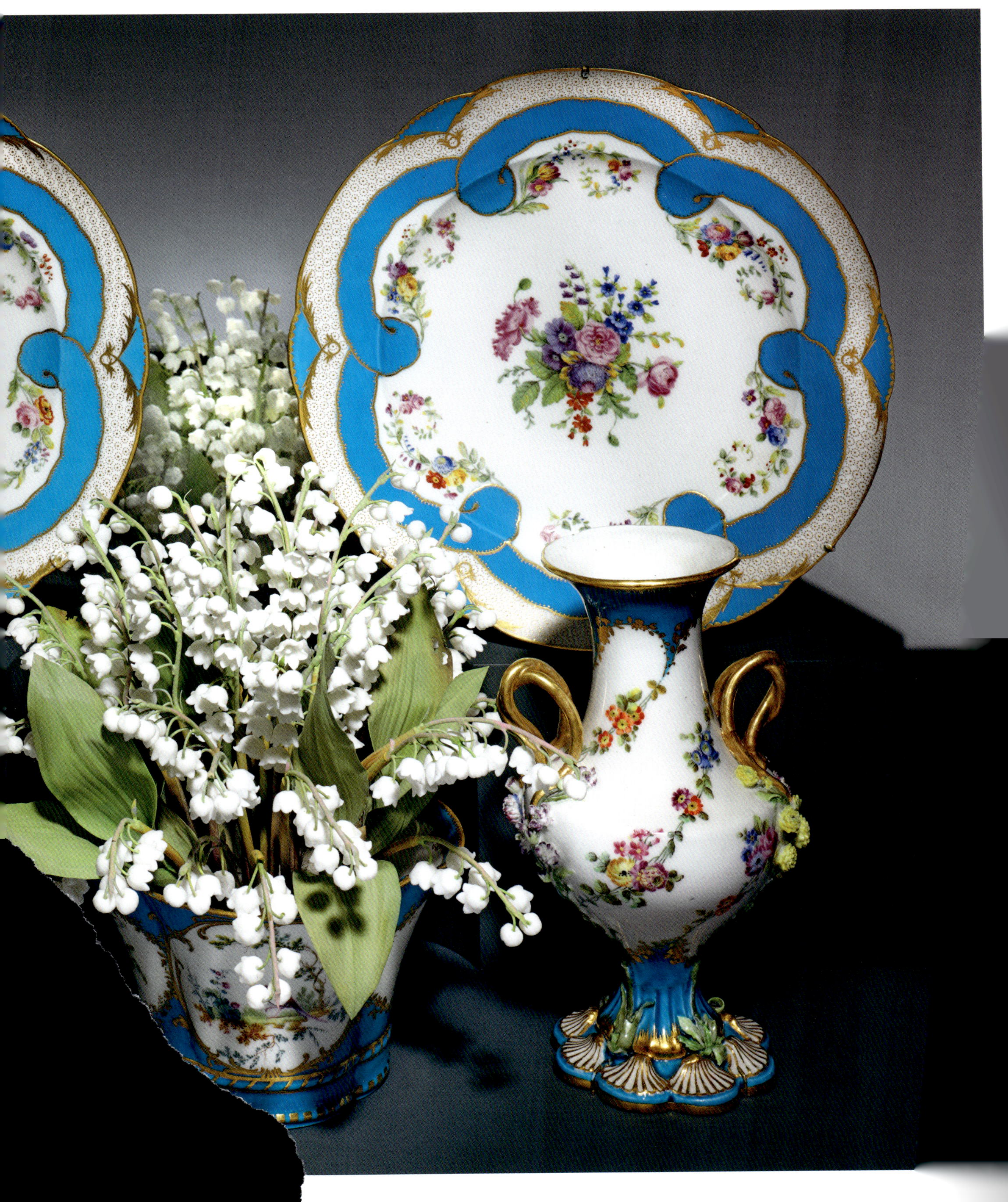

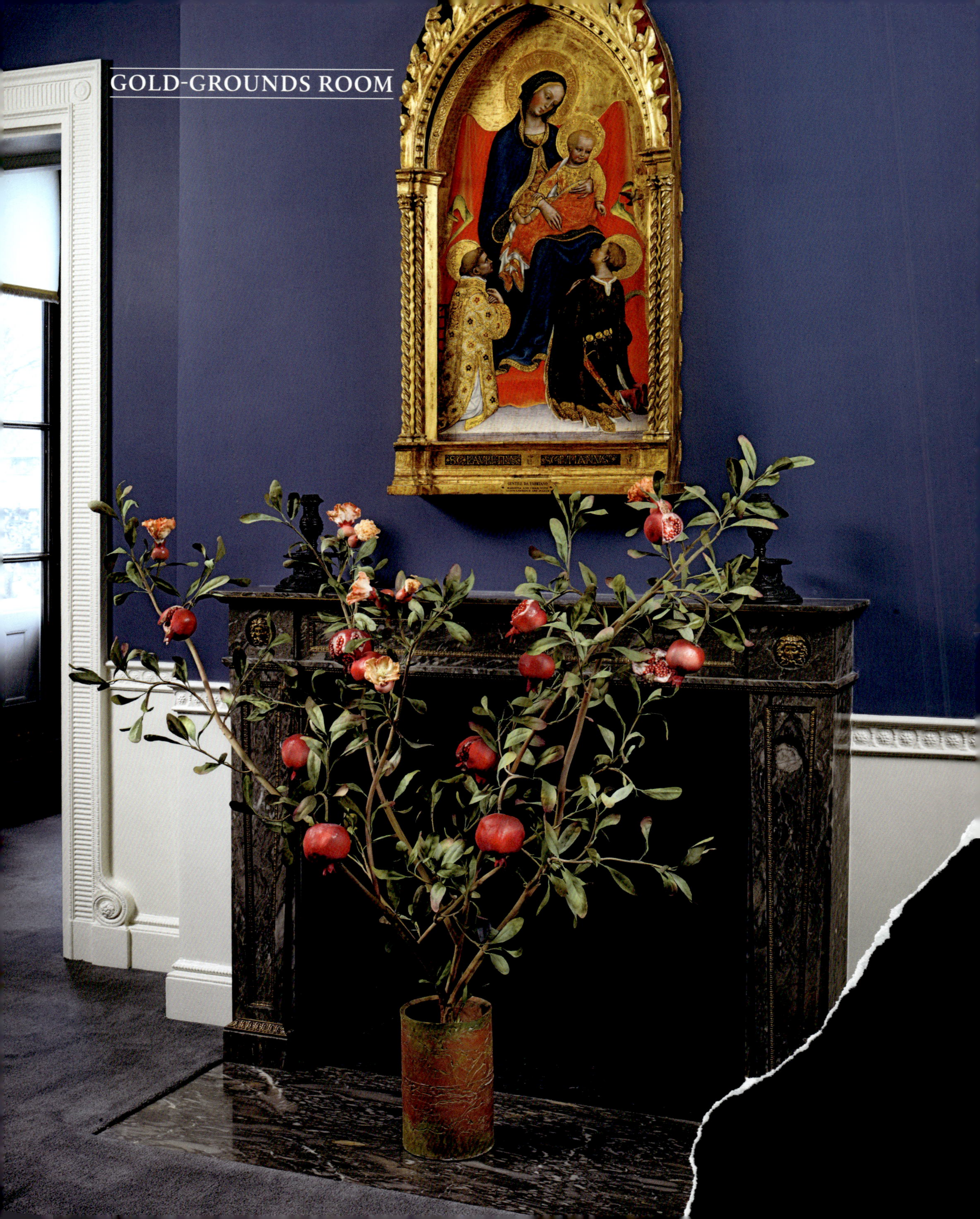

GOLD-GROUNDS ROOM

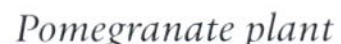
Pomegranate plant

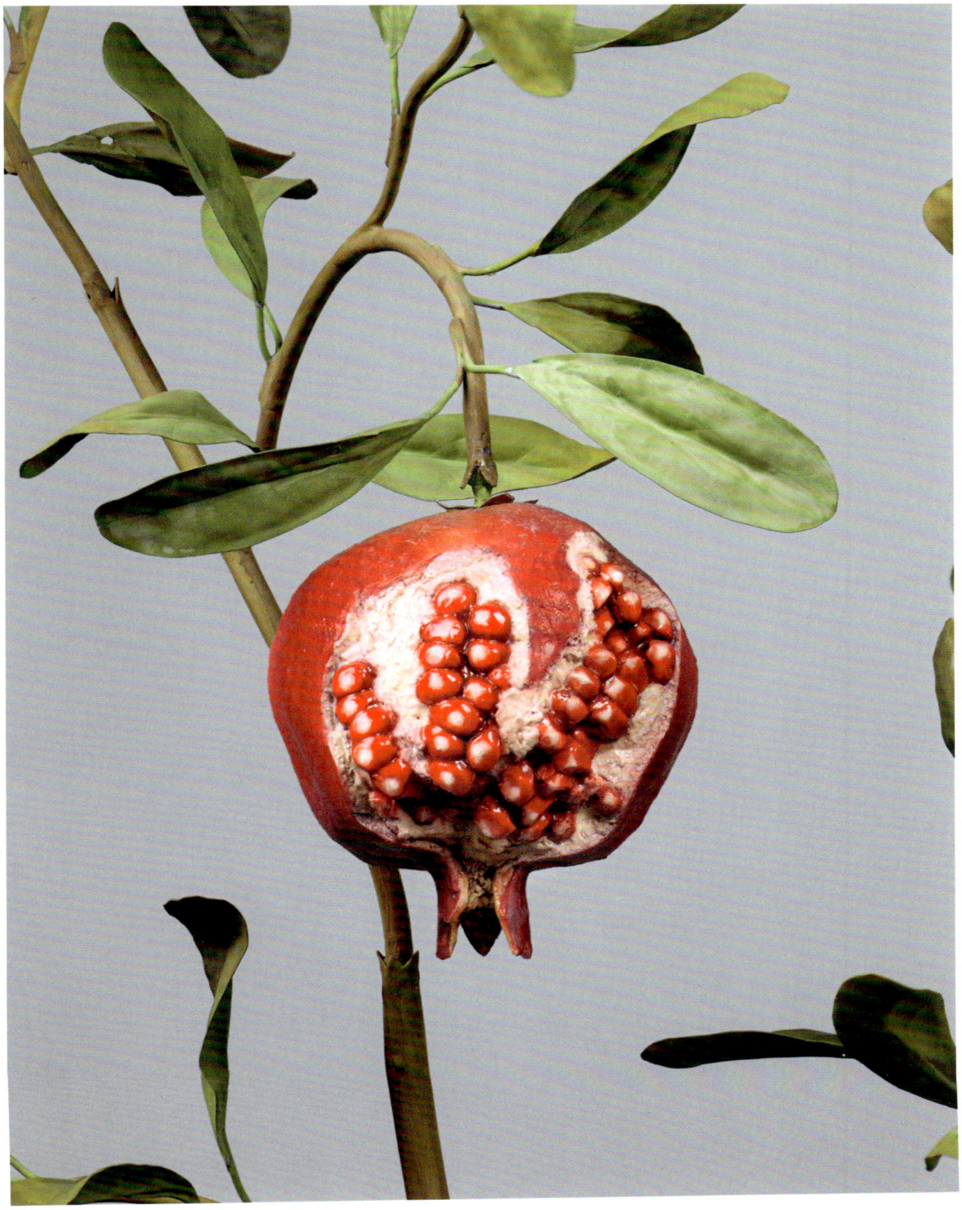

Pomegranate plant

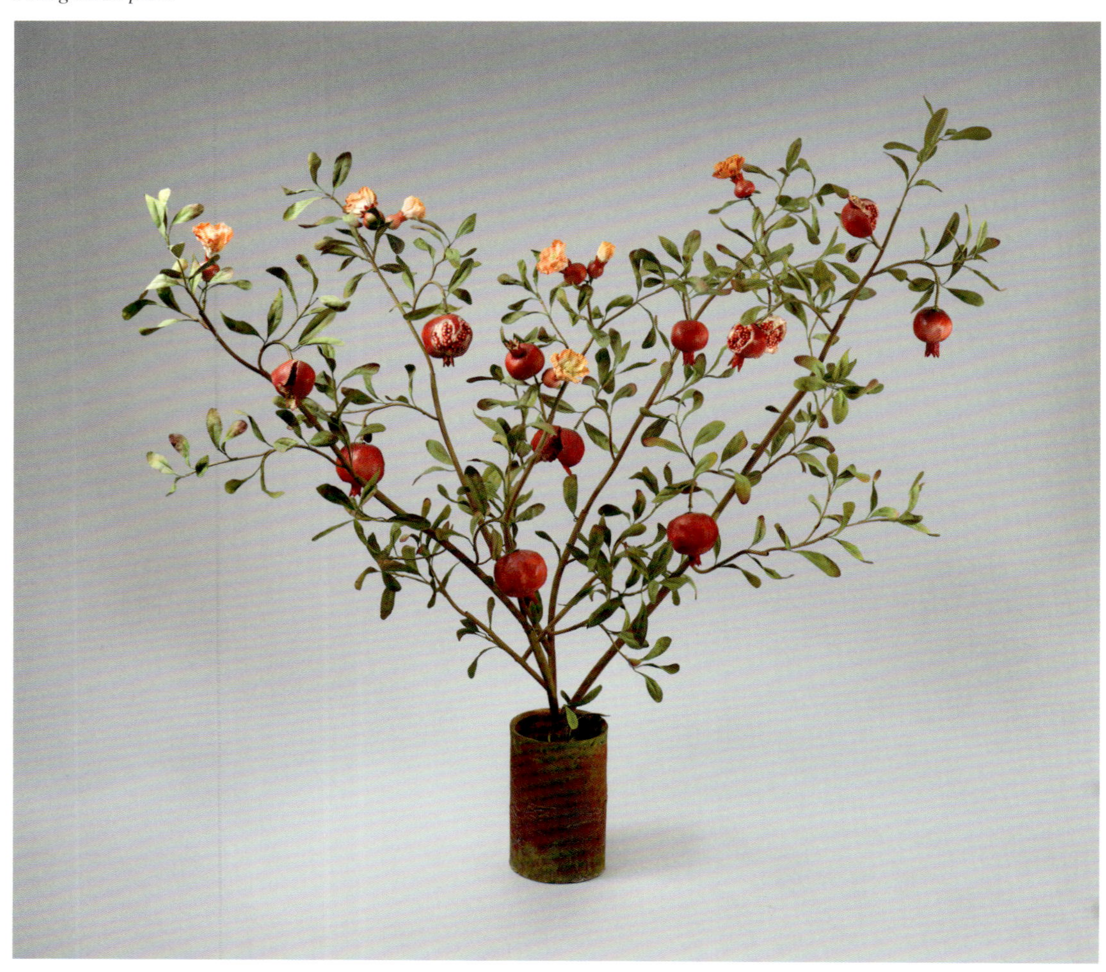

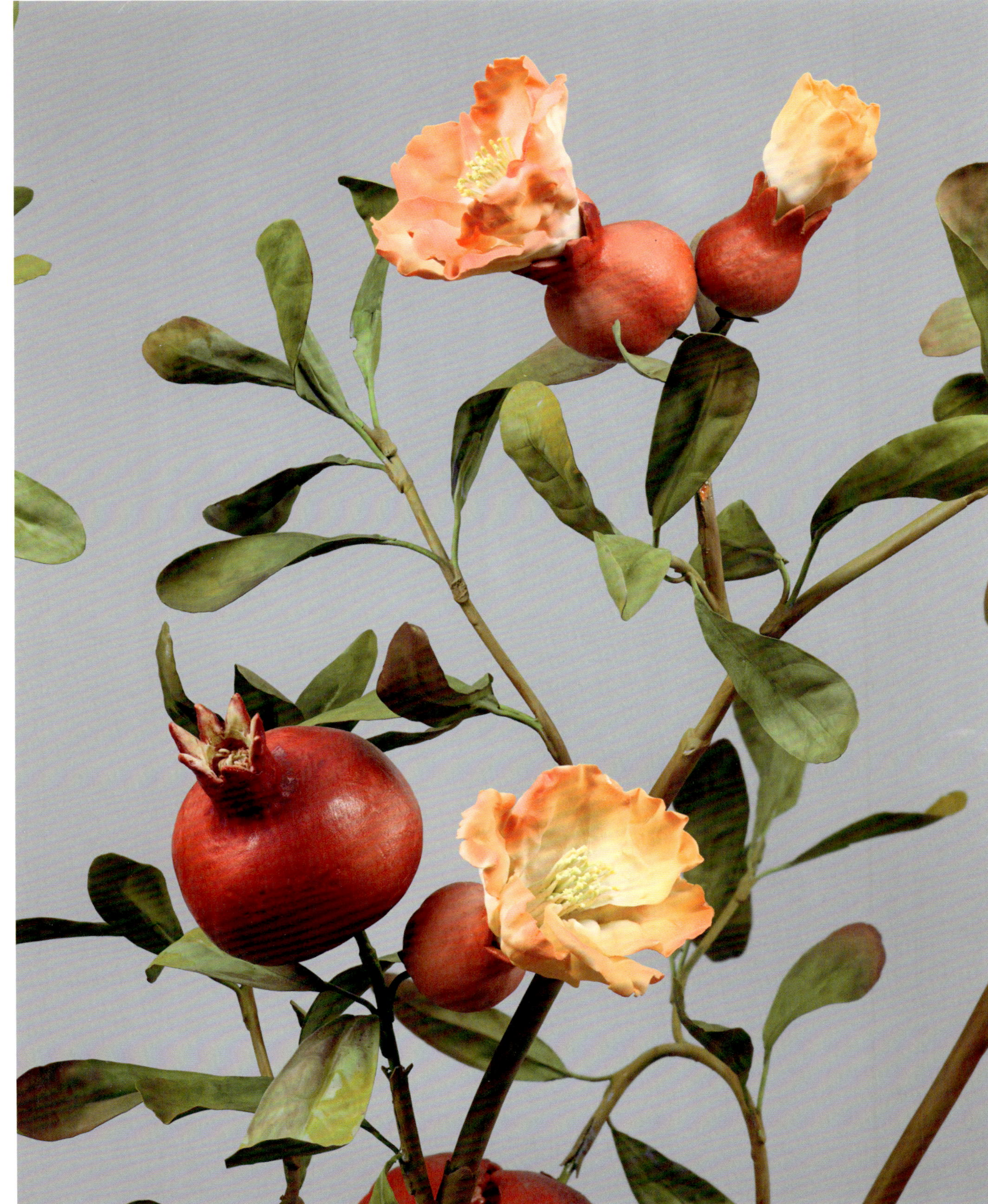

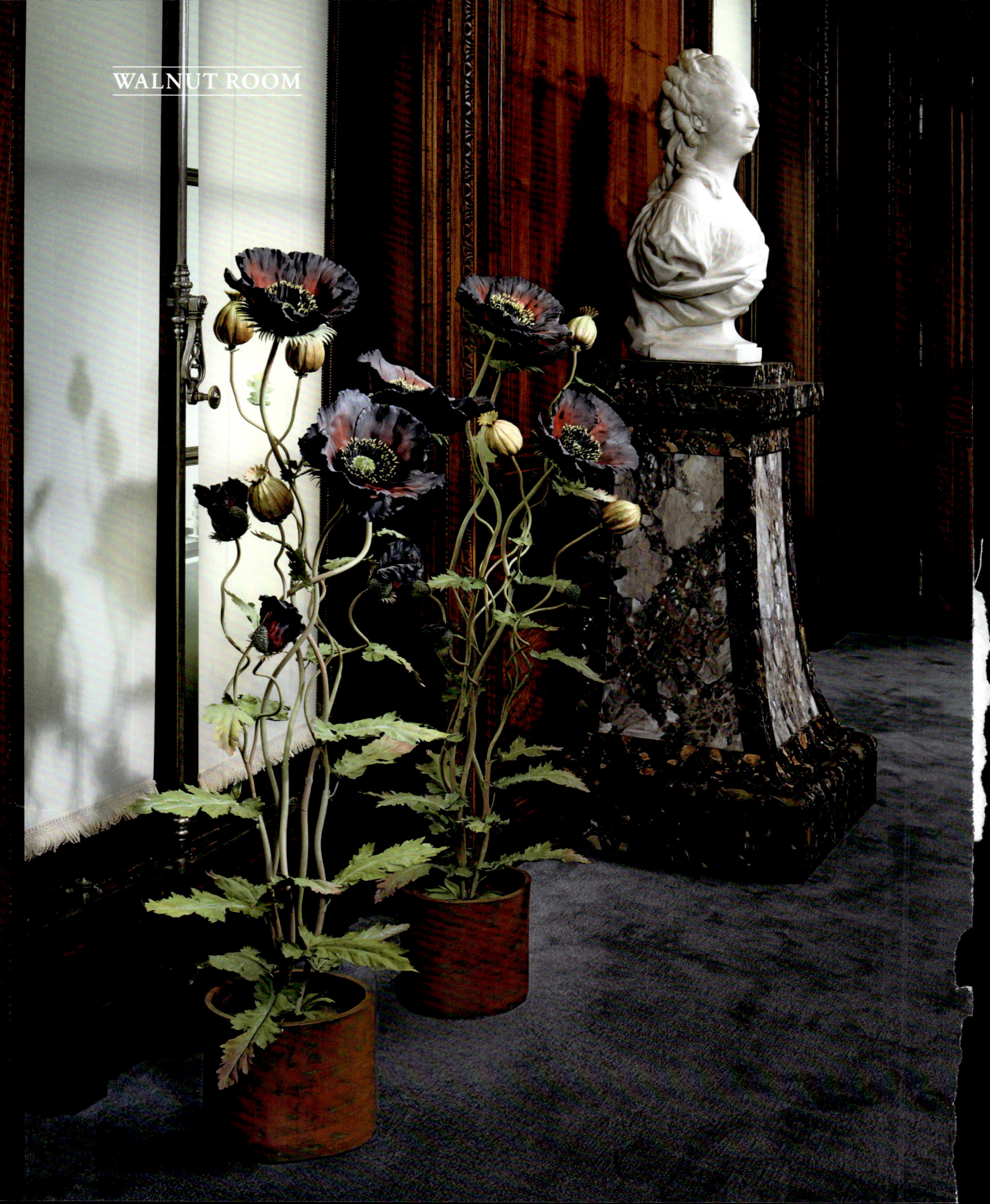

WALNUT ROOM

Black poppies

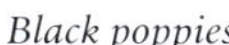

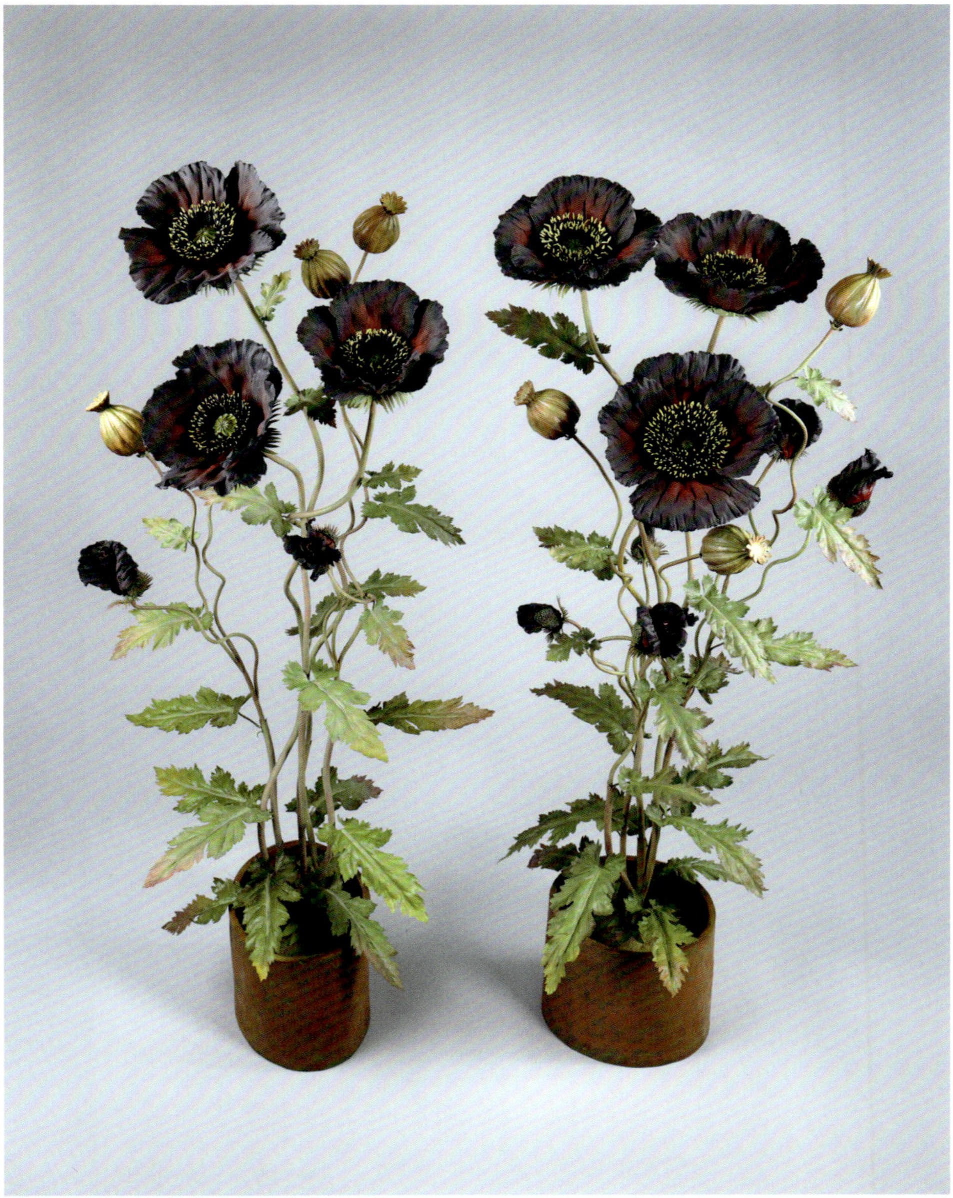

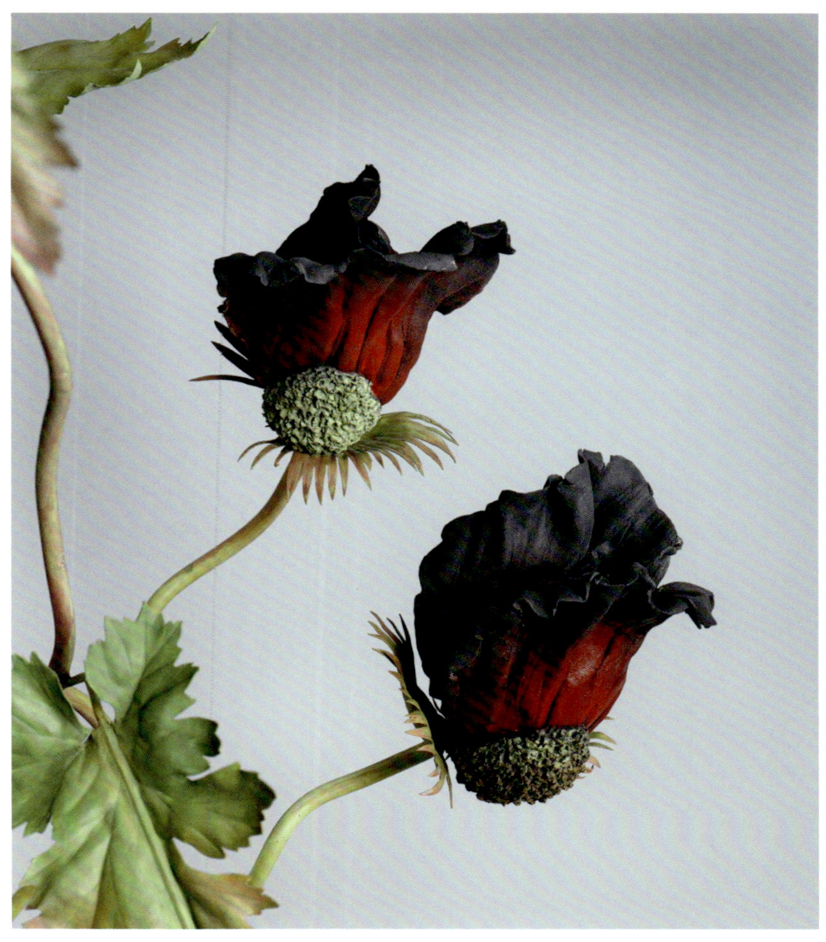

Black poppies

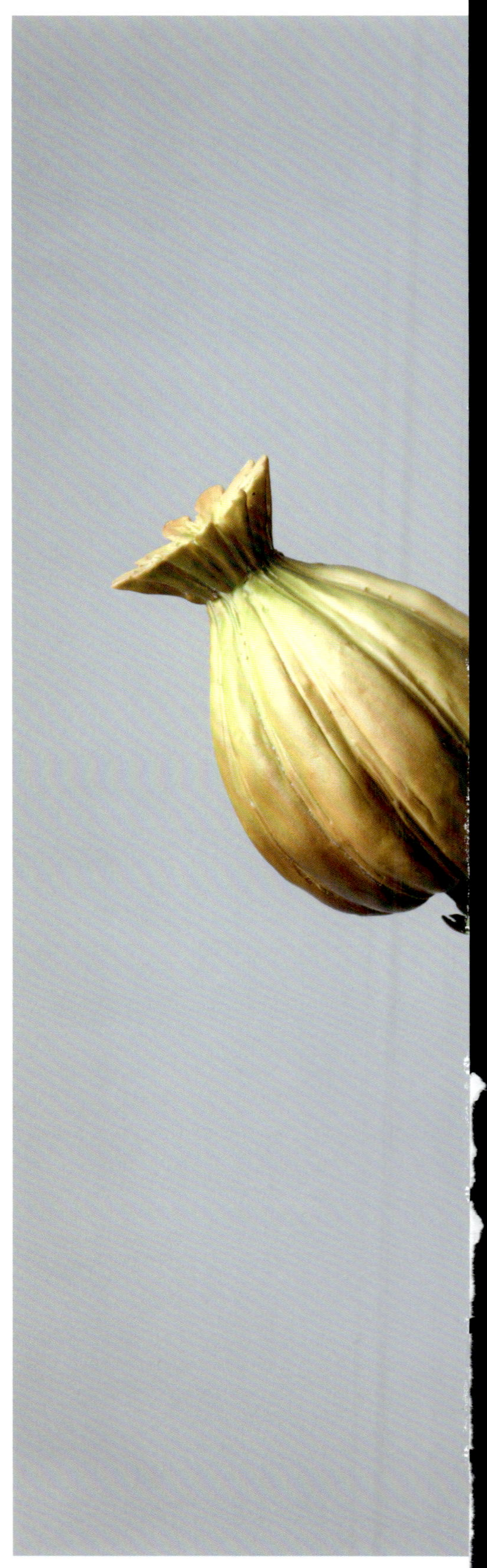

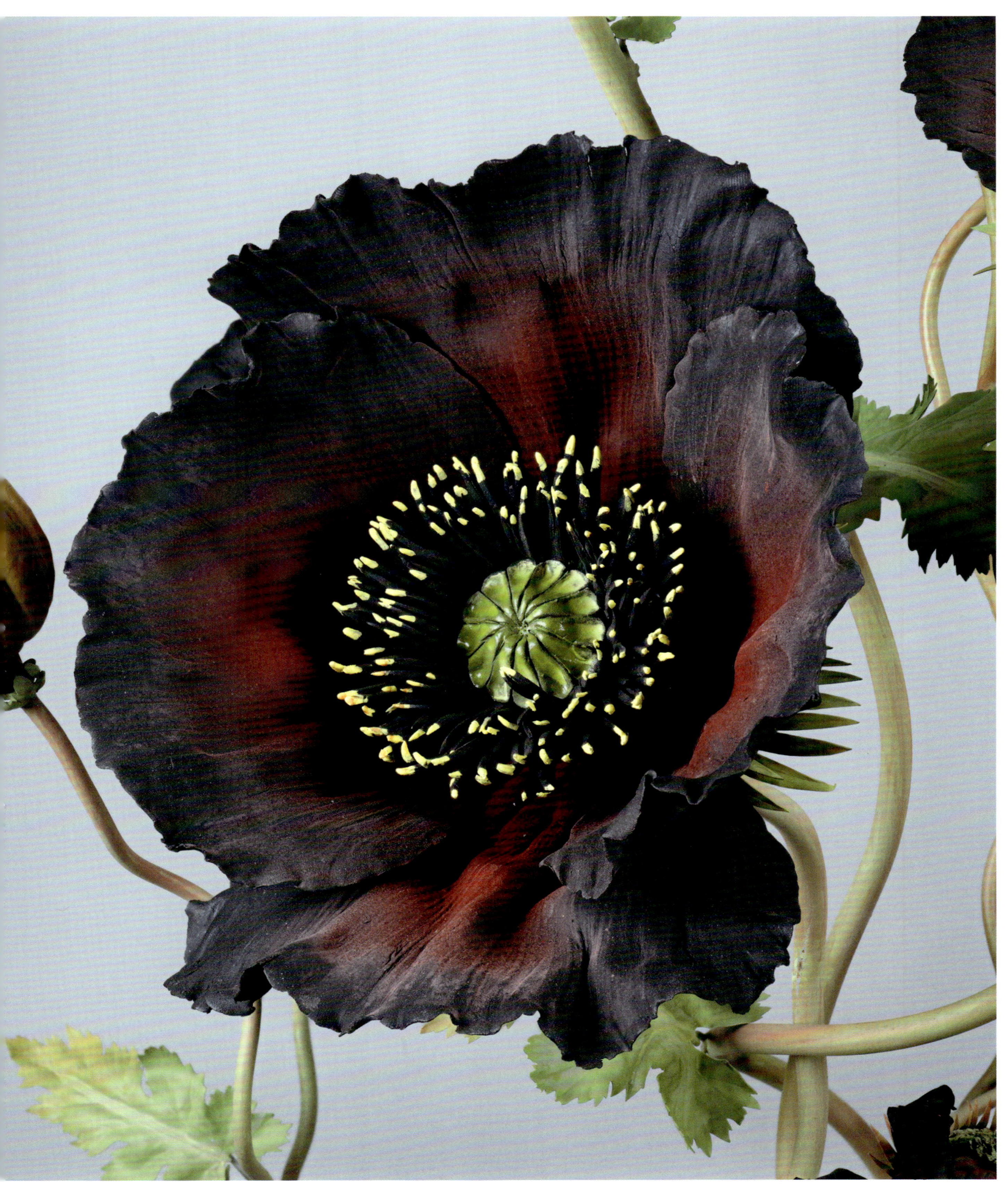